# GENERAL STORE
# COLLECTIBLES

## ·•❖ AN IDENTIFICATION AND VALUE GUIDE ❖•·

David L. Wilson

**COLLECTOR BOOKS**
*A Division of Schroeder Publishing Co., Inc.*

The current values in this book should be used only as a guide. They are not intended to set prices, which vary from one section of the country to another. Auction prices as well as dealer prices vary greatly and are affected by condition as well as demand. Neither the Author nor the Publisher assumes responsibility for any losses that might be incurred as a result of consulting this guide.

ON THE COVER:

**Top Left** — Uncle Sam counter stand-up advertising for Wheatlet Breakfast food. Wilson Collection. $42.00 – 65.00.

**Top Center** — Vapo-Cresolene lamp for whooping cough. Courtesy of Bumpas Emporium. $125.00 – 200.00.

**Top Right** — Child in a swing, 12-month die-cut calendar. Courtesy of Ron Schieber. $175.00 – 275.00.

**Bottom Left** — Buckingham Bright Cut Plug Smoking Tobacco. John J. Bagley, American Tobacco Co. $25.00 – 75.00. Court Royal. San Telmo Mfg. Co., Detroit. Wilson Collection. $45.00 – 85.00.

**Bottom Center** — Michigan cash register, 1906. Courtesy of Bill Navratil. $525.00 – 1,250.00.

**Bottom Right** — Little Goldenlocks and the Three Bears. 10½" x 19¾", 1890 McLoughlin Brothers. Courtesy of Pat McFarland. $525.00 – 1,050.00.

## Searching For A Publisher?

We are always looking for knowledgeable people considered to be experts within their fields. If you feel that there is a real need for a book on your collectible subject and have a large comprehensive collection, contact us.

COLLECTOR BOOKS
P.O. Box 3009
Paducah, Kentucky 42002-3009

Cover design by Beth Summers.
Book design by Gina Lage.

Photography by David L. Wilson with contributions from Patrice McFarland, Chuck Kovacic and Jack Clough.

Additional copies of this book may be ordered from:

Collector Books
P.O. Box 3009
Paducah, Kentucky 42002-3009

@ $24.95. Add $2.00 for postage and handling.

Printed by IMAGE GRAPHICS, INC., Paducah, Kentucky

# ··❖ DEDICATION ❖··

*To my mother,*
  *Jean A. Wilson*

*and to my father,*
  *Lester H. Wilson*

# ··❖ ABOUT THE AUTHOR ❖··

David Wilson has collected country store Americana for more than 24 years. He has been an antique dealer and appraiser, and has operated a museum at California's gold discovery site, Coloma. His extensive general store collection was acquired by the El Dorado County, California, Historical Museum. Mr. Wilson's great-grandfather operated a general store at Watertown, Ohio. Dave has traveled extensively throughout America in his quest to gain knowledge through visits to antique shops, auctions, private collections and museums. He has had the opportunity to talk with a number of "old-timers" who grew up during the era of the old country store and were able to share vivid memories. Dave is a member of the Tin Container Collector's Association, Antique Advertising Association of America, and the Oregon State Historical Society. Mr. Wilson resides in Wilsonville, Oregon, with his wife, Cindy, who shares his interest in collecting, and their two children, Amanda and Grant.

# THE OLD GENERAL STORE

*The wooden sign, through the years of wear, listed the goods we bought with care,*
*Mixing whisks to butter molds, cast-iron stoves when times were cold.*

*Sweet sorghum for a syrup cake, wooden handles for an old leaf rake.*
*Blue pie plates and strong pine tar, honey that filled a green glass jar.*

*Biscuit pans and fresh meat cutters, churns for making country butter.*
*Molasses kegs and one for pickles, sharp saw blades and curving sickles.*

*Natural soap and milking pails, cherry pitters and eight-penny nails,*
*Aladdin lamps and grinding mills, small boxes of Lydia Pinkham pills.*

*Soda crackers and peppermint sticks, chewing tobacco and oil lamp wicks.*
*Old stores had many a tale to tell, of friends and fun, joy and farewell.*

Elisabeth Weaver Winstead

*L.A. Fisher's General Store in Oakley, Kansas. A great photo depicting showcases, Ferry Seed Co. advertising, an advertising clock for Diamond Black Leather Oil, a suspender holder, considerable merchandise, storekeepers, and customers.*
Courtesy of Kansas State Historical Society.

# ⋯◆ TABLE OF CONTENTS ◆⋯

# ··❖ ACKNOWLEDGMENTS ❖··

The completion of this book has been a dream of mine for years. Many people have been of great assistance. My sincere thanks to the archivists, curators, historical associations, and others who were so helpful and generous with their time. For their wonderful help and encouragement, I would like to thank Christie Stanley and Nancy Sherbert of the Kansas State Historical Society; Marilyn Kwock of the Alaska State Library; Marvin J. Mangers, General Manager, Harold Warp Pioneer Village Foundation; Alma Mercer, Lea Bissell, and Leona Parker of the Twinsburg, Ohio, Historical Society, Janice Szabo of the Shelburne Museum in Vermont; The Ohio Historical Society; Beverly Cola and Jack Clough of the El Dorado County, California, Historical Society; and Rose Marie Moore of the Mariposa Museum and History Center, Mariposa, California.

For the generous gift of their time and making their thoughts and collections available, my warmest thanks to Patrice McFarland, John and Mary Jo Purdum, Ron Schieber, Chuck Kovacic, Walter Neal, Bob Brunswick, Bill Navratil, and Scott Bumpas.

I'm also grateful to the late "Bodie" Bill Luther of California. We had many great conversations about collecting over the years and Bill was always eager to share his knowledge. He was a lover of Americana and the Old West with a special twinkle in his eye and a friendly ear. As a person in his eighth decade, his enthusiasm for collecting was unrivaled.

Thanks also to my wife, Cindy, who has provided encouragement, enthusiasm, technical assistance, and a great deal of patience.

Special thanks to Chuck and Jennie Melville for introducing me to country store collectibles and offering their friendship.

To the many wonderful collectors and dealers I have known over the years, thank you for adding so much to my knowledge and, most of all, the many unforgettable times and pleasant experiences.

My interest in old mercantile stores started when I was a child. My family loved to go fishing and we had the opportunity to make trips to many locations, including remote areas of Canada. I can recall visits to a number of stores and trading posts. Many had a fascinating variety of original artifacts on display. Several had original showcases, cheese cutters and some actually used an ancient National Cash Register. Through the eyes of a curious child, these old-time stores were a real treat. A trading post we visited in Canada was only accessible by boat and I can recall Native Americans bringing furs to the storekeeper for sale or barter. I also found out later in life that my mother's grandfather operated a small general store in Watertown, Ohio. Years later, I visited Watertown. The old store is still there but not operating and the small village appears much like it must have been around the turn of the century. Merely a slight application of imagination can take you back to 1900 as you walk the tree-shaded main street.

I also had the opportunity to take a trip with my Dad to Elizabeth, West Virginia, and see where he spent much of his early boyhood. The original Roberts Mercantile Store is still in business and operated by the descendants of the founder. The store was established in the nineteenth century and retains much of its original appearance. My father has vivid memories of the local old-timers sitting on the store's porch exchanging stories and farm information while smoking a pipe or chewing and whittling away with a Barlow knife. As Dad and I walked through the store, two things entered my mind. Dad was born in 1913 and made frequent visits to this store throughout his boyhood. He walked those same well-worn wooden floors that we were walking. Many of the original fixtures remained from Dad's boyhood and he could recall them. He pointed out the counter where he brought eggs to trade when he was only five years old. We recently celebrated Dad's 80th birthday but he can remember his "grow-ing up" days in Elizabeth as if those years were a recent event.

It seems like I have always had a fondness for American history, the Old West and country stores. In my travels around this glorious country, I have been privileged to see the remains of old general stores in a number of ghost towns of the Old West as well as operating stores in villages and hamlets of today's America. I have a great deal of gratitude for the many people who have preserved and protected country store collectibles over the years. My collection includes some tins that were manufactured in the late 1870's that survived in remarkable condition. It is truly amazing to consider that many hands and places have touched the "life" of a tin but over 100 years has not diminished the condition! Collectors, dealers, interior decorators, museums, and others have now become the preservationists to assure the continued life and vitality of old store items.

The past thirty years or so have seen country store items go from the category of old junk to priceless collectible. Sale prices have approached $100,000.00 for a single advertising sign, over $20,000.00 for a tin container and $16,000.00 for a board game. This price range is certainly at the very top of the value scale but clearly demonstrates what has happened in a relatively short period of time. What does the future hold? My personal feeling is that desirable country store items will remain highly sought after but prices may well fluctuate with the ultimate range of values subject to much speculation. Because of the rapid rise of prices over the past several years, collectors and dealers are much more price conscious than back in the "good old days" of collecting. Talk to any long-term collector or dealer and you will hear some incredible stories about prices and values. On the plus side, now that old store collectibles have gained a great deal of respect, it is more probable that the artifacts will be given very special care and preservation for future generations to enjoy. A collector's nightmare is to reflect on all of the choice general store collectibles that were thrown in the dump or destroyed prior to the time of such prominence and desirability.

I became "hooked" on country store Americana back in 1968. There were several pioneers in the field before that. I recall going to the home of Chuck and Jennie Melville who continue to be collectors and dealers of early American furniture, country store and other fine antiques. When I saw the display in their California home, I became a serious collector and faithful customer. Chuck and Jennie are very special dealers and they became friends. They were always on the lookout for me and sold items at very fair prices. My collecting enthusiasm was an adventure filled with the excitement of discovery but very rough on the wallet.

My vacations and trips were centered around country store memorabilia searches that have taken me from California to Maine. I found some great spice tins in the high mountains of Silverton and Ouray, Colorado. A wonderful oak "bean-counter," 12 feet in length, was located in Salt Lake City. Tobacco tins and coffee grinders along with some early advertising items were discovered in shops on the rural roads of Missouri and Kansas and while driving through fabulous fall foliage in Vermont and New Hampshire. Along the way, I have met some wonderful people for which I'm truly thankful. I've always looked at antique collecting in general as a modern-day adventure with some similarities to prospecting in the Old West. You can never be certain what might turn up and, if nothing does, the pure pleasure of looking, meeting new people and seeing new places is reward enough. There can be some poignant moments. I recall traveling the back roads of Kansas several years ago and coming to a town that was obviously settled in the nineteenth century. It had a very impressive town square with a number of attractive and substantial commercial buildings. Sadly, many of the old establishments were out of business. I also noticed that much of the town's population were older citizens. When I spoke with the elderly lady who owned the local antique shop, she explained that most of the younger people had moved away and that the once prosperous town was in the middle stages of becoming a ghost town. She told me that most of the younger generation had little interest in becoming part of the local farm economy. She commented that the old mercantile store was once so crowded on Saturdays that farm families expected to spend a fair amount of time picking up the goods they needed. I found a few things for my collection and left that small Kansas town with a new appreciation for changing America.

Another trip brought a surprising and pleasant discovery. Just outside Durango, Colorado, was an old ranch with a building proclaiming "Museum." I find it very difficult to pass up a local museum so I quickly pulled off the road and was greeted by the owner, a very gregarious gentleman of 80+ years. We entered his private museum and a large portion of the display area was devoted to a re-created old-time store. He was very proud of his collection and talked enthusiastically about attending auctions and looking other places for additions to his impressive store display. The years may have separated us but we were kindred spirits as we talked "old stores." He lived on the family's original homestead and was a real inspiration. Later during that trip, I camped in the mountains above Georgetown, Colorado. Magnificent mountains and a wonderful time. Can you ask for anything more?

I have seen private country store collections numbering thousands of items and I have also been a guest in homes where just a few cherished collectibles were present. That is what makes collecting such a fun pastime. There is something for everyone. For relatively modest amounts of money, a person can acquire some very enjoyable collectibles. The old general store offered so much: tins, trade cards, patent medicines, posters, billheads, tobacco items, and store fixtures, to name a few.

Every collector of store material has probably had the fantasy of moving back the clock. If a "Back to the Future" wish could be granted, we would all like to be placed in a circa 1890 general store with enough cash to "buy" to our hearts content. Since that is not possible, I hope to give the reader a realistic substitute through the pages of this book. I have made an effort to include collectibles that are generally available. I have also made an effort to include numerous collectibles that have not appeared in other books.

The outstanding color and graphics of country store material have always intrigued me. Tins, advertising posters and store giveaways offer an incredible variety of the lithographer's art. Going hand-in-hand with all of this are the wonderfully illustrated games that were produced during the glory years of the general store. This book will bring a number of these games to the reader. For color and interest, they should certainly have the attention of the country store collector.

My love of country store Americana continues to grow. I welcome hearing from those of you who would like to share your enthusiasm and mutual interests. It has been a pleasure to bring this book to you and it is my hope that you enjoy every page!

## ••❖ A Note on Pricing ❖••

Determining a fair market value for unique and scarce collectibles can be a dilemma. There are so many factors that have a direct influence on the ultimate price. Demand for and condition of the item are the two major considerations. In addition, the motivations of the buyer and seller, geographical location, economic conditions, and overall strength of the antiques market at a given time can contribute to selling price.

The best tool for pricing that one can use is an average range price. If a specific Diamond Dye cabinet, for example, brings $1,850.00 at auction and within days the same cabinet in similar condition is purchased at an antiques show for $1,250.00, what is the correct value? Did one purchaser pay too much and one too little? Situations similar to this occur frequently. Since country store collectibles are in limited supply, selling prices often reflect the buyer's enthusiasm to acquire a piece, even at the risk of paying too much.

This book makes every effort to give the collector a general idea of the range of values for country store items. The prices are based on collectibles found in good to excellent condition.

One comment about the cash registers illustrated in this book. These machines can be found in working condition with evidence of many years of hard usage. The prices can be very attractive because the machines are mechanical and the collector can't be certain how long the cash register will continue to function. If, on the other hand, a decision is made to purchase a completely renovated machine with a "factory new" appearance, the price will reflect condition. The machines illustrated in this book have undergone extensive renovation and such work is costly.

The values assigned are based on the author's knowledge as a long-time collector, talking with dealers and other collectors, attending auctions, following the trade journals, visiting antique shops and attending a number of shows.

# Chapter One
## ⊰ THE HISTORIC GENERAL STORE ⊱

Welcome to the incredible world of the old general store! There was probably never a stronger institution in the history of America. The real glory years only lasted about 60 years and covered the period roughly from 1870 to 1930. During that time, the old stores served crossroad villages, hamlets, and small towns throughout the populated United States. General merchandise stores served as centers of trade to sparse populations, provided a popular meeting spot, frequently offered post office service and fulfilled a variety of other needs. The stores were clearly a link to the major cities and provided goods that reminded patrons of the civilization they may have left behind. A store was vital to the needs of the local population as well as a provider of numerous services.

In addition to fulfilling his major role as storekeeper, the enterprising merchant was often a politician, banker, accountant, lawyer, insurance representative, and, perhaps most important, a genuine diplomat. The owner of a general store had great knowledge of his customers, their likes and dislikes, problems and financial situations. This was vital knowledge since many transactions involved credit and barter.

The general store was often a two-story building with the second floor used for storage, merchandise display, or perhaps a meeting place for a local church or fraternal organization. The front of the store had two large display windows which featured a hodge-podge of merchandise that went long periods of time without being changed. Everything from hats,

*Rodgers Brothers Grocers, 1870's, in Topeka, Kansas. Rodgers Brothers provided home delivery with a fleet of wagons and fine horses.* Courtesy of Kansas State Historical Society.

shoes, tools, lamps, and crockery were displayed in the windows. An ambitious merchant would change the window display with the arrival of a large stock of new goods or perhaps at Christmas and spring.

Most general stores had platforms or wooden sidewalks built in front of them. The platform cut down on dirt that was tracked into the store and also provided a convenient loading platform for customers.

Historical research has provided evidence that the stores ranged from a very small mercantile establishment with limited goods and frequently just a few sales away from economic disaster to the very large, soundly operated stores with a huge variety of goods and unlimited optimism. Such a store was the Peter Robidoux Store in Wallace, Kansas. Mr. Robidoux started his enterprise with a barrel of whiskey and a box of cigars and developed it into a giant emporium offering everything from fancy pearl-handled Colt six-shooters to a complete suit of clothes. It was the largest establishment of its kind in operation between Kansas City and Denver.

Inside, the typical general store was cluttered with piles of merchandise and crammed shelves. Space always seemed to be at a premium. When a particular item was requested, the storekeeper often had to take a moment to think about the location. Many stores prided themselves on the ability to come up with just about anything a customer had in mind. A storekeeper was once challenged to come up with a coffin and was able to locate one in his storage shed. The store often had circular stools for the comfort of lady customers as they looked over the stock of yard goods and related items. Some stores would open as early as 5:00AM to prepare for the day's business and welcome the early bird. Saturday was "store day" for families in the area and a day to sell or barter farm produce. Few general stores specialized in anything but instead offered a wide range of goods.

The storekeeper often preferred wearing black sateen sleevelets over his shirt from cuff to elbow. He was the best informed of all residents because he eventually had contact with just about everyone on a fairly regular basis. Shopping was an event looked forward to as a time for socializing as well as buying.

The wise storekeeper understood that it was necessary to have a good "handle" on the needs and wants of his customers. Purchasing was done by visits to wholesale houses or ordering through the drummers that made their rounds. If the merchant truly had a good understanding of his customers, he could select the proper inventory. If wrong decisions were made, the items became slow movers or "shelf-stickers" and money out of the storekeeper's pocket. This

*The P. Robidoux Store of Wallace, Kansas, circa 1888. This mercantile business touted itself as "Dealer In Everything" and it certainly was. Peter Robidoux started his store in Wallace with a barrel of whiskey and a box of cigars and his first store was a simple tent. He eventually built the business to the biggest general store between Kansas City and Denver. Business continued to boom until the financial panic of 1893. There was finally a day when not one single piece of merchandise was sold. Robidoux closed for good, leaving $20,000.00 worth of goods on the shelves.* Courtesy of Kansas State Historical Society.

could later prove to be the cause of failure of the store. The larger general stores did make an effort to meet every need. Shotguns, ammunition, shoe blacking, china, crockery, confections, tobacco, buggy whips and books were available. Often, a brisk business in funeral goods brought in some money and the store proprietor often served as the local undertaker. Being appointed postmaster was a plum that just about every country store owner sought out. Naturally, this brought people into the store on a regular basis, bringing about additional sales.

The mercantile trade in America first offered primarily the necessities of life because few people had extra resources for luxuries. After the Civil War, there was a substantial growth in factories, and economic conditions began to enable people to afford some luxuries. The old rule had been that purchases were made only if the item could not be made or raised. As the economy of America grew, the storekeeper was still faced with customers who carefully pondered over every purchase and caused a great deal of impatience with the store proprietor.

Stores were often dark and rather gloomy places. Most of the wall space was taken up by shelving so there were few windows to let in light and fresh air. Some historians feel the shopkeepers preferred this situation because it made the goods more difficult to inspect. The closed-in environment of the store captured the many smells that mingled together to create something very distinctive. Fresh leather goods, kerosene, coffee beans, cheese, dry goods, tobacco, and spices all contributed to that great aroma.

In time, general stores did make some effort to arrange goods by departments. On one side

*Alaska Mercantile Co's. branch store "Emporium." Nome, Alaska, October 1st, 1906.* Courtesy of Alaska State Library.

of the store would be the dry goods section with fresh bolts of cloth, ribbon, thread, silk, corsets, paper collars, and suspenders. Near the front of the store would be a section devoted to hard candy in jars, tobacco, cough drops and patent medicines. Stationery, pens, paper, books and valentines would be kept in a case. The grocery section offered coffee, tea, spices, crackers, cheese, and molasses among other items.

There was a strong demand for cheap goods and this demand helped bring about some sharp practices by suppliers, stores, and customers. Plain beans were mixed with coffee, starch was used to stretch out baking powder, and water was added to milk. Sawdust found its way into oatmeal and chocolate was doctored with flour. Gypsum was placed into pepper and flour was cut with plaster and potato starch. Deaconing the apples was also a common practice. The top of the barrel or container was simply topped off with the largest and best fruit. It was unfortunate that the merchant usually got the blame and loss of character and goodwill. There were times, however, when the merchant

was as guilty as his supplier, or the customer who tried to trade adulterated milk or honey, and pass off old eggs as fresh.

To the merchant's favor, it was necessary for him to often extend credit and the majority of accounts were settled satisfactorily. Many families survived on the goodwill and trust of the storekeeper during times of economic problems. The merchant also needed to possess the ability to trade properly for country produce. Butter, eggs, honey, poultry, vegetables, fresh fruit, hides, chestnuts, black walnuts, and feathers frequently found their way to store counters.

Most stores had a cellar that was reached by a trap door at the rear of the store. The cellar was a keeping place for barrels of syrup, molasses, turpentine, and kerosene. Crocks of butter, stocks of rope, wood encased cheeses, and a jumble of boxes, crates, and other merchandise were stored in the basement. In the earlier days of the general store, most merchandise arrived in bulk, which created a need to store kegs, barrels and wooden boxes of every sort.

*Unidentified grocery store in Valley Falls, Kansas.* Courtesy of Kansas State Historical Society.

*Reno Cash Store, Reno, Nevada. Owners Robert Nelson & Ross Petersen. Circa 1900.* Wilson Collection.

*J. Harris General Merchandise, "dealers in dry goods, clothing, boots and shoes, groceries, bacon, lard, cheese, notions and fancy goods. The establishment promises to give fair goods in exchange for produce at low cost." The store also houses the post office. Unknown location on the Plains. Circa 1880.* Wilson Collection.

*A general store and post office on the Western frontier. The store was hastily erected and the proud owners are optimistic about the future. Circa 1880.* Wilson Collection.

As you can imagine, the general store was also a favorite loafing place for those who seemed to have nothing important to do and preferred sitting around the store stove swapping stories and telling tall tales. When the weather became more accommodating, "center-stage" was adjourned to the front porch. The storekeepers seemed to tolerate these individuals as long as hands didn't make too many free trips to the cracker or raisin barrels.

The storekeeper was frequently a willing participant in many of the discussions that took place within the store. His wisdom and knowledge of the outside world was respected. His wit and ability to keep up with his customers is also well-documented. An example was the customer who asked for an item and was told the price was $5.00. The shocked customer stated that the general store in the community a few miles away quoted a price of $3.50 but did not have the particular item in stock. To that, the storekeeper replied that his price was also $3.50 when he did not have it in stock but, since he did, the price was $5.00!

It is difficult to put a value on the importance of the general store in the daily life of the community it served. It was considered vital as a provider of goods and services as well as a place to socialize and catch up on all the latest news. The old country store reflected prosper-

ous times and was a link to places like Paris, New York, Chicago, Denver, and San Francisco. World geography was also represented. Tea from China, allspice from Jamaica and the East Indies, ginger from Africa, cottons from Calcutta, coffee from Brazil and tropical fruit from the West Indies were just a few of the products representing exotic locations. The storekeeper performed numerous personal services for his patrons including weighing their babies on the store scale, writing letters, drawing up simple contracts and serving as the arbiter of a dispute. A fine cigar or the latest in fabrics could be just as available at the crossroads store as in Denver or Chicago. That was very comforting to those living in isolated areas. The old store helped raise the generations and when the time came, provided the necessary goods for caskets and mourning.

By 1930, the golden age of the rural general store was coming to an end. The institution had been caught up in the march of progress. The major factor was the extended usage of the automobile and improved highway system. This broadened the shopping area of rural folk and the roads led to towns and cities with a greater selection of merchandise. The invention of the telephone made it less necessary to visit the local store. Orders could be called in and many of the merchants offered home delivery. Rural

*Custer's Store at Arkalon, Kansas. This fantastic interior shot is a great example of the old general store around the turn of the century. Just look at all of the wonderful collectibles! "Everything under one roof" was certainly true for this store.*
Courtesy of Kansas State Historical Society.

*George D. Davis, Grocer, Tacoma, Washington. A classic photo including the owners, an old-timer on the porch and two youngsters taking their leisure. Circa 1890.* Wilson Collection.

*Interior of a general store circa 1890. Location unknown.* Wilson Collection.

*L.K. Chamberlin & Co., Twinsburg, Ohio.* Courtesy of Lea Bissell.

*A crowd gathers outside the McCreery Store to witness the first automobile in Twinsburg, Ohio, being driven by Dr. R.B. Chamberlin.* Courtesy of Lea Bissell.

free mail delivery and parcel post opened the door to catalog companies like "Monkey Wards" and "Shears & Sawbuck." Many general store owners with a post office became increasingly depressed as they mailed off their customers' requests for orders to the catalog firms. Pleas for loyalty had some impact and long-time customers felt good about continuing a long-term business relationship. But the majority of people were impressed with the range of merchandise and low prices offered by the mail-order houses. The offer of "satisfaction guaranteed" was also welcomed. If this wasn't enough, specialty stores were growing by leaps and bounds. No longer was it necessary to purchase everything in one location. Specialty stores offered more variety, the latest merchandise and attractive prices. Time had caught up with the old general store. Its once proud position

as a supplier of everything to everyone had been diminished to a place to conveniently pick up a loaf of bread or a soft drink. The general store along with the horse and buggy, once so important to daily life, were no longer needed. In many ways, we can envy those who had the opportunity to experience the golden age of the general store.

*The delivery truck of McCreery's Store, Twinsburg, Ohio.* Courtesy of Lea Bissell.

### Original Photographs

Photographs of exteriors and interiors of the old general store are a growing collector's area. Nothing reflects the true feeling of the old mercantile establishments more faithfully than original photos. They offer documentary evidence of just what these stores looked like as well as the astounding variety of merchandise they stocked.

There is something special about looking at a Diamond Dye cabinet, Enterprise Coffee grinder, Calumet Baking Powder clock, or a Corticelli Spool Silk cabinet in the original setting. The old false-front exteriors, customers, storekeepers, children, and horses add just that much more. Just as every store was different, every photograph is unique and individual.

Early store photographs can run the entire spectrum of price ranges. A fairly common view with nothing extraordinary about it can sell for as low as $5.00 – 10.00. An original photo of a general store in Tombstone, Arizona, circa 1870, for example, could bring hundreds of greenbacks. Size, subject matter, clarity, and condition of the photograph will have an impact on value.

Most quality photographs can be purchased in the $25.00 to $125.00 range.

I truly enjoy the old photographs and made a special effort to include as many of them as possible in this book. In my conversations with collectors, dealers, and historians around the country, it was apparent that many share my fervor.

*An unidentified general store, circa 1890. Note the numerous boxes, barrels and crates. The proprietor is posing with his young boy. The store is well-equipped with a number of showcases.* Wilson Collection.

*The interior of the McCreery Store, Twinsburg, Ohio.* Courtesy of Lea Bissell.

*Exterior of the McCreery General Store, Twinsburg, Ohio.* Courtesy of Lea Bissell.

*Nichols Store in Osborne, Kansas, 1890's.* Courtesy of Kansas State Historical Society.

*Whitcraft's Store, Bath, Ohio. Whitcraft's was one of the largest general stores in the area and carried everything from toothpicks to farm implements.*
Courtesy of Leona Parker.

*Exterior of the Bishop General Store, Twinsburg, Ohio.* Courtesy of Leona Parker.

*Interior of the Bishop General Store, Twinsburg, Ohio. Mr. Bishop and his son are pictured circa 1920's. Mr. Bishop learned much about the mercantile trade while clerking at the Whitcraft Store in Bath, Ohio, on wages of $25.00 a month.* Courtesy of Leona Parker.

*The Asa Knight Store started in the early nineteenth century and operated as a general store until 1862 in Dummerston, Vermont. Now on the grounds of Old Sturbridge Village, Massachusetts.*

*The James P. Mosier General Store in Idaho. This exterior photo of the store declares it offers groceries, shoes, dry goods and gents furnishings.* Wilson Collection.

*An interior scene of the James P. Mosier Store in Idaho.* Wilson Collection.

*Another interior scene, of the dry goods section of the Mosier Store.* Wilson Collection.

*An unidentified general store in Ohio. It appears that the store has some Christmas decorations. The large coffee grinder is a Star Mill and appears in the next chapter.* Wilson Collection.

*Alaska Mercantile Company Dry Goods Department, Nome, Alaska, 1907.* Courtesy of Alaska State Library.

*A view of the Gagliardo Store in the collection of the Mariposa Museum & History Center, Mariposa, California. This store started in Hornitos, California, in 1854 and was operated by the same family until 1960.*
Courtesy of Mariposa Museum & History Center.

*The Treadwell Store, the Alaska-Treadwell Gold Mining Company, Treadwell, Alaska. This company store stocked all the necessities of life including such rare treats as imported ripe bananas.* Courtesy of Alaska State Library.

*Another area of the Treadwell Store showing the store's post office and extensive stock of goods.* Courtesy of Alaska State Library.

*Interior of unidentified general store at the turn of the century.* Wilson Collection.

*Interior of unidentified general store in Missouri.*
Wilson Collection.

*Exterior of the Tuckaway General Store, Shelburne Museum, Shelburne, Vermont.*
Courtesy of Shelburne Museum.

*Interior of the Tuckaway General Store, Shelburne Museum, Shelburne, Vermont.* Courtesy of Shelburne Museum.

*The candy counter of the Tuckaway General Store, Shelburne Museum, Shelburne, Vermont.* Courtesy of Shelburne Museum.

*Exterior of the People's General Store, Harold Warp Pioneer Village, Minden, Nebraska.* Courtesy of Harold Warp Pioneer Village.

*Interior of the People's General Store, Harold Warp Pioneer Village, Minden, Nebraska.* Courtesy of Harold Warp Pioneer Village.

*The old general store located in Ghost Town at Knott's Berry Farm, Buena Park, California.* Courtesy of Knott's Berry Farm.

*MAIL-ORDER SPECS printed by The American Optical Company, 1942. This copy of the original painting captures a part of everyday life at the old general store. $95.00 – 120.00.* Wilson Collection.

*Store proprietor "Penrose Collins" ringing up a sale in the general store exhibit of the El Dorado County Historical Society, Placerville, California.* Courtesy of Jack Clough.

*A larger view of the general store collection, El Dorado County Historical Society, Placerville, California.* Courtesy of Jack Clough.

### Billheads

In order to carry a wide variety of merchandise, it was necessary for the country store proprietor to do business with a number of suppliers. There were wholesalers and manufacturers for such diverse goods as crackers, coffee, glass and lamps, firearms and ammunition, boots and shoes, soaps and perfumes, starch, hardware, crockery, and stove blacking, to name a few. The merchant carried on a stream of communication with his various suppliers. I have come across a large volume of such correspondence and it is a fascinating glimpse at the business practices of the nineteenth and early twentieth centuries. These documents further my appreciation for the skills that were necessary to operate a successful general store.

The business letterheads of yesteryear also contain enchanting examples of design and typography. They have generally been overlooked as a country store collectible but they offer mercantile history and colorful graphics at a very modest cost.

Any paper material relating to the business of the old general store should be of interest and value to collectors. This includes the old colorful commercial billheads as well as other related ephemera. It is possible to find billheads that relate directly to tin containers and other advertising items, or other specific products.

The collector can locate billheads for less than $1.00. Prices will rise dramatically if the billhead contains significant historical information or has origins in the old American West.

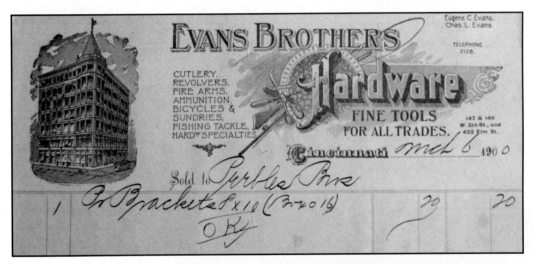

*Evans Brothers Hardware, Cincinnati, Ohio, March 6, 1900. Dealers in fine tools, cutlery, revolvers, fire arms, ammunition, bicycles & sundries, fishing tackle and hardware specialties. $5.00 – 8.00.* Wilson Collection.

*Portland Coffee & Spice Co., Portland, Oregon, May 23, 1898. Dealers in tea, coffee, spices, baking powder, extracts, etc. This would have been at the time of the Klondike Gold Rush and many of this company's products were shipped to the Klondike to bring some comfort to the miners. $4.00 – 7.00.* Wilson Collection.

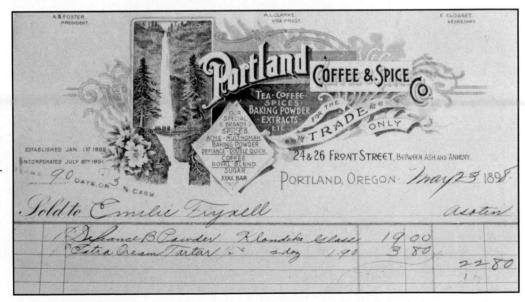

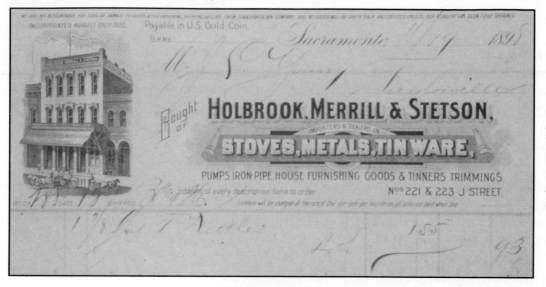

*Holbrook, Merrill & Stetson, Sacramento, California, November 19, 1898. Dealers in stoves, metals and tin ware. $5.00 – 8.00.* Wilson Collection.

*H.R. Droste & Co., Cincinnati, Ohio. Coffee roasters, spice grinders and mustard manufacturers. February 8, 1901. The company letterhead also indicates that it manufactured the celebrated Snow Drift Baking Powder. $4.00 – 6.00.* Wilson Collection.

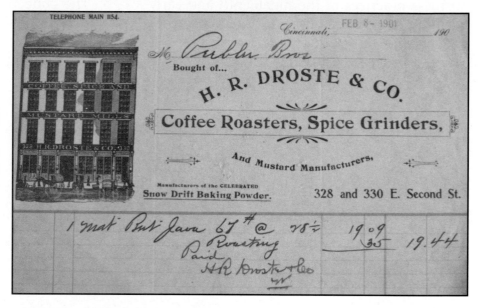

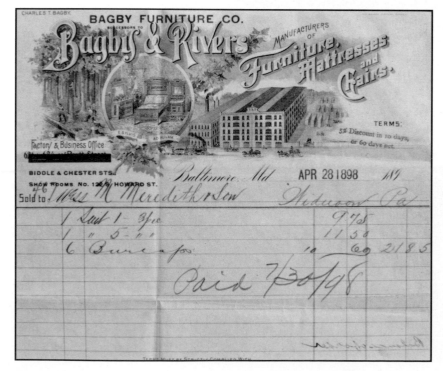

*Bagby Furniture Company, Baltimore, Maryland, April 28, 1898. Manufacturers of furniture, mattresses and chairs. $4.00 – 7.00.* Wilson Collection.

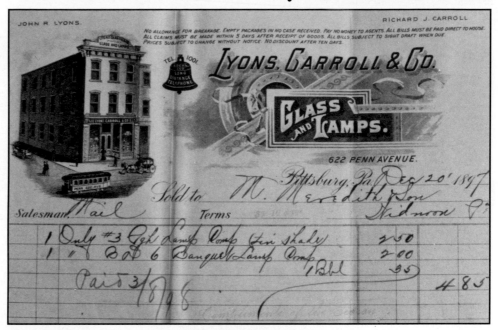

*Lyons, Carroll & Co., Pittsburgh, Pennsylvania, December 20, 1897. Dealers in glass and lamps. $3.00 – 5.00.* Wilson Collection.

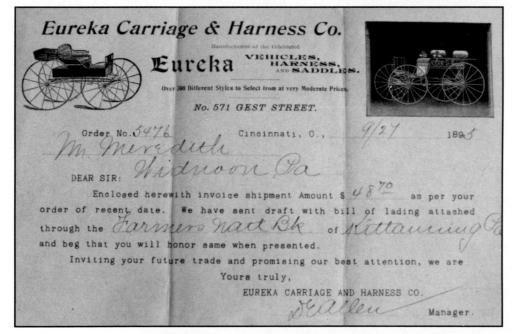

*Eureka Carriage & Harness Co., Cincinnati, Ohio, September 27, 1895. Manufacturers of the celebrated Eureka carriage with over 300 styles to select from. Also a provider of harness and saddles. $3.00 – 6.00.* Wilson Collection.

*The Henry Roever Company, Cincinnati, Ohio, March 2nd, 1900. Dealers in soaps and perfumes. $3.00 – 5.00.* Wilson Collection.

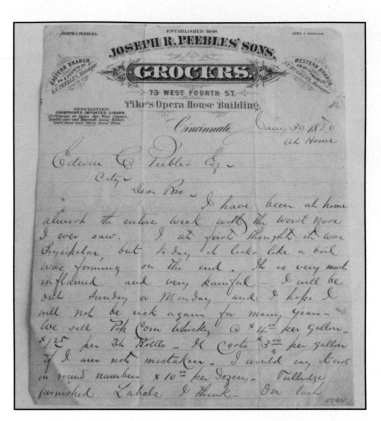

*Joseph R. Peebles' Sons, Pike's Opera House Building, Cincinnati, Ohio, January 30, 1880. Joseph Peebles is writing to his brother who operated another branch of the business. $2.00 – 4.00.* Wilson Collection.

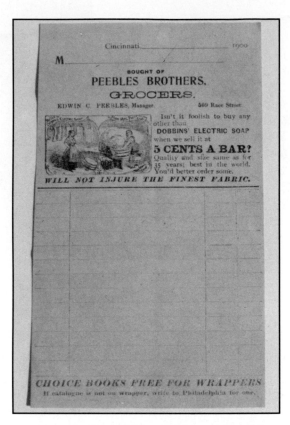

*Peebles Brothers Grocers, Cincinnati, Ohio. Free invoice forms provided by Dobbins Electric Soap. $2.00 – 4.00.* Wilson Collection.

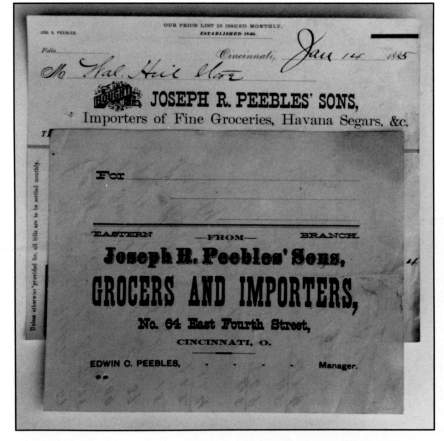

*Two items of correspondence from Joseph R. Peebles' Sons, Cincinnati, Ohio. The bottom document is the reverse of a store invoice. $2.00 – 4.00.* Wilson Collection.

*Tippecanoe Wheel Works, Tippecanoe City, Ohio, August 29, 1872. Manufacturers of carriage wheels, hubs, spokes, and bent material. $2.00 – 5.00.* Wilson Collection.

*Billheads of A. Janszen & Co., Wholesale Grocers, and Evans Brothers Hardware. $4.00 – 7.00.* Wilson Collection.

*Small books like these were provided free of charge to store customers so they could keep a personal record of their accounts. $6.00 – 12.00.* Wilson Collection.

# Chapter Two
## ❖ STORE FIXTURES ❖

During the raw frontier years, storekeeping required a minimum of fixtures to operate. Some crude counters, hasty shelving and a stock of goods opened the door for business. By 1870, things had clearly changed for the rural stores in many areas. There were manufacturers to provide custom counters, showcases, and whatever else the merchant might require to continue on his path to prosperity.

A large bright-colored coffee grinder was necessary to serve the growing trade. Manufacturers included Enterprise of Philadelphia and rival Star Mill manufactured in Philadelphia by The Henry Troemner Company. Others included Elgin; Landers, Frary, and Clark; and Ferry-Morse. This particular instrument was not held in high esteem by the store clerk. Grinding several pounds of coffee beans was not a favored duty. Probably nothing represents the character of the old stores as much as the old coffee grinder. When this magnificent symbol of the mercantile trade had outlived its usefulness, thousands were discarded at the dump or sold for scrap metal. It is amazing that so many have survived. It is increasingly difficult to locate one with the original "tomato-red" or other color paint, ornate decals, and all parts still intact. Many an old storekeeper would be amazed at the value a fine coffee grinder commands in today's antique market.

*A Number 5 Enterprise Coffee Grinder with wooden drawer. $525.00 – 800.00.* Courtesy of John and Mary Jo Purdum.

*Star Mill counter coffee grinder manufactured in Philadelphia, Pennsylvania, by Henry Troemner. This mill is a "Number 12" and was patented November 25, 1884. The grinder is in remarkable condition and retains all parts, original colors, and decals. There are decals of an arrow, horseshoes, whip, and spurs. This coffee grinder saw service in the old mining town of Sumpter, Oregon. 41" high. $2,500.00 – 3,200.00.* Wilson Collection.

*Large Enterprise counter-model coffee grinder with removable tin scoop. $850.00 – 1,300.00.*
Courtesy of El Dorado County Historical Society, Placerville, California.

*A trio of small Enterprise Coffee Grinders in great condition. There are two Number 5's and one Number 4. $525.00 – 800.00 each.* Courtesy of John and Mary Jo Purdum.

A variety of scales was necessary to weigh everything from tea to babies. Some great examples are available to the collector. Many scales were painted in attractive colors and featured stencils and other eye-catching designs.

As more products came on the market and the store became more cluttered, the storekeeper looked for some methods to bring order to his establishment. A good solution to aid in organizing goods were showcases. German silver and oak-framed showcases were offered by a number of manufacturers in places like St. Louis, Chicago, and Cincinnati. As business prospered, a number of manufacturers of a variety of goods offered free showcases to merchants in exchange for an understanding that the showcases would be prominently displayed and the specific product enthusiastically promoted to customers. Many of the showcases had the etched name of the company on the glass to further identify their products. Dye cabinets, spool cabinets, coffee bins, spice caddies, and other fixtures were offered to the storekeeper free of charge.

*Large store scale manufactured by the Perfection Scale Company, New Canaan, Connecticut. Patent date April 1, 1879. $375.00 – 550.00.* Wilson Collection.

*Small candy scale manufactured by the Chicago Scale Company. $165.00 – 250.00.* Wilson Collection.

I have a copy of a letter dated 1897 from Wells & Richardson Company of Burlington, Vermont. Collector's recognize the company as the manufacturer of Diamond Dyes and beautiful display cabinets. The letter offers to provide the Sharp & Fleming Mercantile Company an oak dye cabinet provided a specified quantity of dyes is purchased. With one gross of Diamond Dyes, the beautiful cabinet with a bright-colored embossed scene on the door is included. Wells and Richardson also promises a "nickel-silver showcard and a nice line of advertising handouts." The company literature indicates that the cabinet can be finished in cherry, antique oak, black walnut, or ebony, with one swinging door opening in front and two sliding doors in the rear. Popular colors of the day were indigo blue, plum, violet, turkey red, and Easter dyes. The cabinets came in several designs featuring women, children, the ages of life, and other themes. They certainly attracted attention in yesteryear's store as they do to today's collector.

*A wooden Diamond Dyes counter display showcase. $275.00 – 575.00.* Courtesy of John and Mary Jo Purdum.

*A beautifully illustrated Diamond Dyes cabinet, Wells & Richardson Company, Burlington, Vermont. $1,650.00 – 2,300.00.* Courtesy of John and Mary Jo Purdum.

This cabinet is generally referred to as "The Governess" or "School Teacher." Diamond Dyes, Wells & Richardson Co., Burlington, Vermont. $1,200.00 – 1,850.00. Courtesy of John and Mary Jo Purdum.

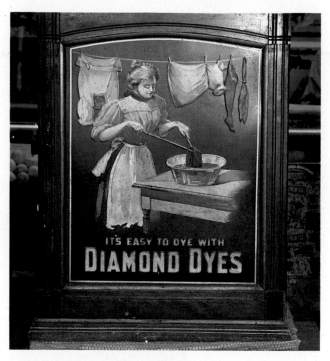

Diamond Dyes Cabinet with an illustration of a lady dyeing clothes. Wells & Richardson Company, Burlington, Vermont. $1,350.00 – 2,400.00. Courtesy of John and Mary Jo Purdum.

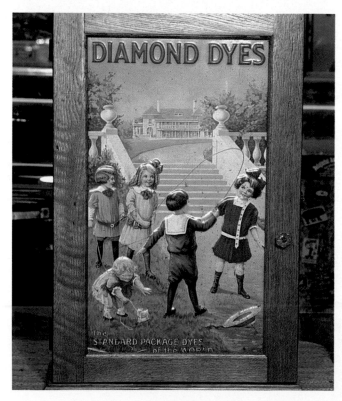

Diamond Dyes "Jumping Rope" by Wells & Richardson Company, Burlington, Vermont. $850.00 – 1,200.00. Courtesy of John and Mary Jo Purdum.

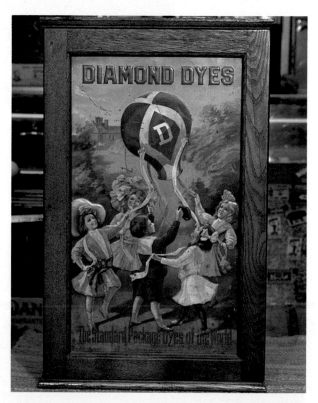

Diamond Dyes oak cabinet with children playing with a colorful balloon. Wells & Richardson Company, Burlington, Vermont. $800.00 – 1,150.00. Courtesy of John and Mary Jo Purdum.

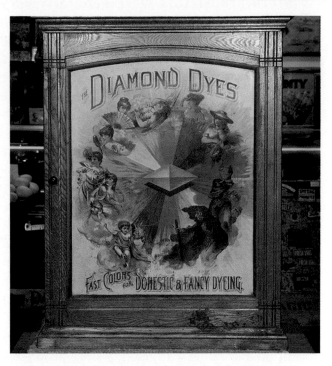

*Diamond Dyes "Court Jester" cabinet finished in cherry. Wells & Richardson Company, Burlington, Vermont. $650.00 – 850.00.* Courtesy of John and Mary Jo Purdum.

*Diamond Dyes "Evolution of Women." Wells & Richardson Co., Burlington, Vermont. $625.00 – 850.00.* Courtesy of John and Mary Jo Purdum.

*Diamond Dyes "The Baby." Wells and Richardson Company, Burlington, Vermont. $875.00 – 1,300.00.* Wilson Collection.

Store proprietors were generally very shrewd businessmen and were blessed with a great knowledge of human nature. In spite of these admirable qualities, many merchants were very susceptible to the sales pitch of the cash register salesman. Many a store with a modest operation boasted an ornate cash register with features that often exceeded needs. There was something about these machines that sent a strong success message to customers along with the distinct "tingle" every time a sale was made.

A saloon-keeper in Dayton, Ohio, was experiencing a problem with "shrinking receipts" and decided to invent a machine that would aid in eliminating the problem. Dishonest cashiers did not welcome the machine and many honest cashiers felt the machine was a negative reflection on them. James Ritty enjoyed success with his invention and James Patterson, a store proprietor in Coalton, Ohio, heard of the "thief preventor" and ordered a machine from Ritty. Patterson also enjoyed success with this "silent partner" but felt

it was crudely made and could be greatly improved. Mr. Patterson eventually acquired the necessary interests and started the foundation of The National Cash Register Company.

The first machines were made available in the 1800's. From 1888 to 1895, there were 84 companies reported to be selling cash registers. Only three companies eventually survived with National Cash Register doing the majority of business.

The demands on metal usage during World War I brought an end to the ornate brass and silver-plated cash registers.

Close examination of an early cash register can demonstrate why owners of mercantile stores were so attracted to them. The brass cabinets are intricate and beautiful. The machine was almost like a shrine to the money it was made to hold. Storekeepers could select from many designs and have their names or store names custom-made to fit the machine. They could consider a very basic model or go to the top of the line.

*A great collection of restored National Cash Registers.* Courtesy of Bill Navratil.

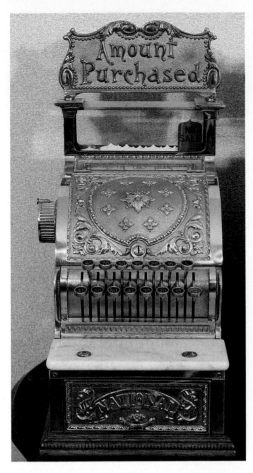

*National Cash Register Model 50 done in Renaissance Pattern. Equipped with a clock. 1902. $750.00 – 1,600.00.* Courtesy of Bill Navratil.

*National Cash Register Model 215. Rings to 50¢. Copper oxidized over brass. Fleur de Lis pattern. Circa 1900. $650.00 – 1,500.00.* Courtesy of Bill Navratil.

*National Cash Register with extended base. Marble coin shelf. Dolphin pattern. Rings to $1.00. 1907. $750.00 – 1,750.00.* Courtesy of Bill Navratil.

*National Cash Register with raised fancy till. Fleur de Lis pattern. 1908. $750.00 – 1,600.00.* Courtesy of Bill Navratil.

*National Cash Register in nickel over cast iron. Brass key checks. Ionic pattern. 1902. $650.00 – 1,450.00.* Courtesy of Bill Navratil.

*The well-used ornate brass and wood drawer of a National cash register.* Courtesy of Bill Navratil.

*National Cash Register Model 442. Electric. 1912. Equipped with a crank handle in the event of a power failure. Rings to $9.99. A good model for a general store. $650.00 – 1,350.00.* Courtesy of Bill Navratil.

*Michigan Cash Register. Rings to $1.00. 1906. $525.00 – 1,250.00.* Courtesy of Bill Navratil.

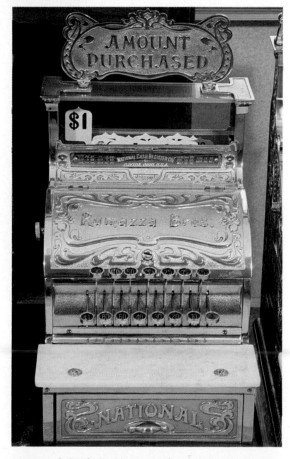

*National Cash Register with custom "Rumazza Brothers" inscription. Art Nouveau pattern. Made by Toledo Cash Register Company. 1902. $750.00 – 1,600.00.* Courtesy of Bill Navratil.

*National Cash Register Model 15 with clock. Finished in Renaissance with the heaviest pattern offered. The machine is a total adder and rings to $1.00. 1899. $700.00 – 1,500.00.* Courtesy of Bill Navratil.

*National Cash Register Model 30 in nickel. Has a total adder with detail code. Rings to $1.00. Has fancy bar above drawer. Also equipped with a "Patterson Pull" which was also called "devil-head." 1897. $750.00 – 1,600.00.* Courtesy of Bill Navratil.

*A side view of the Model 15.* Courtesy of Bill Navratil.

*Left: National Cash Register Model 5. Brass and bronze with nickel-plated drawer and custom name plate. 1895. $750.00 – 1,600.00.* Courtesy of Bill Navratil.

*Right: National Cash Register Model 5, H. Goldberg name plate. 1902. $700.00 – 1,500.00.* Courtesy of Bill Navratil.

*National Cash Register Model 251. Rings to 50¢. 1906. $750.00 – 1,500.00.* Courtesy of Bill Navratil.

*National Cash Register. Displays "Toll Paid" plaque. 1904. $700.00 – 1,500.00.* Courtesy of Bill Navratil.

Beautiful store clocks with prominent advertising were also available as well as silk cabinets, needle and pin cabinets, whip and broom holders, tobacco cutters, and store lamps. The makers of None Such Mincemeat provided a particularly attractive store lamp. If a merchant could achieve a certain sales volume, there were many store fixtures to be claimed free of charge. Often, the fixtures were simply given outright to a merchant in exchange for a promise to "push the goods."

When the store was properly outfitted with the many fixtures of the day and business was good, the busy merchant could take a moment or two to reflect on his good fortune and look forward to a promising future.

*A silver-plate embossed hanging store lamp of the type in general use prior to gas or electricity. The store would have several of these to provide light. They came equipped with a tin shade. $350.00 – 625.00.* Courtesy of John and Mary Jo Purdum.

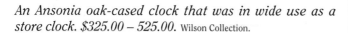
*An Ansonia oak-cased clock that was in wide use as a store clock. $325.00 – 525.00.* Wilson Collection.

*A Plains buffalo bronze that once posed proudly on a store-keeper's desk in Deadwood, South Dakota. $375.00 – 500.00.* Wilson Collection.

*An American eagle that occupied a spot on the top of a storekeeper's roll-top desk in Dodge City, Kansas. $35.00 – 65.00.* Wilson Collection.

*A storekeeper's oak roll-top desk and chair from Sutter Creek, California. Many general store proprietors favored this desk because of the generous space it afforded and the fact that it could be quickly locked so important papers could be kept confidential when the desk was not in use. $2,500.00 – 3,350.00.* Wilson Collection.

*A typical store stove. Fuels used were wood and coal. $275.00 – 350.00.* Courtesy of El Dorado County Historical Society, Placerville, California.

*A turned-maple hat stand. $38.00 – 65.00.* Wilson Collection.

*A store mannequin dressed in long-johns and cast iron high-top shoes. $200.00 – 325.00.* Courtesy of John and Mary Jo Purdum.

*A razor strop case, $450.00 – 675.00, and oak-framed collar case, $900.00 – 1,750.00.* Wilson Collection.

*Metal-framed collar case. $650.00 – 875.00.* Courtesy of John and Mary Jo Purdum.

*An oak-framed collar case. $1,250.00 – 2,500.00.* Courtesy of John and Mary Jo Purdum.

*Children's Hickory Garters wooden cabinet with an illustration of a child's dog "assisting him" with his new garters. $375.00 – 550.00.* Courtesy of John and Mary Jo Purdum.

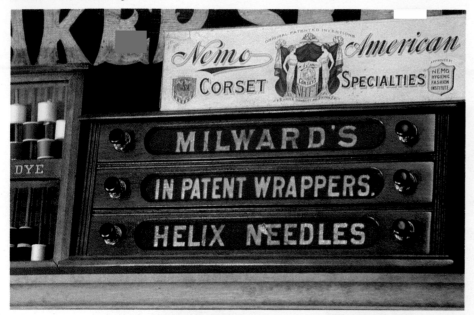

*Nemo American Corset Specialties container, $25.00 – 40.00. A Milward's Helix Needles box, $450.00 – 900.00.* Courtesy of John and Mary Jo Purdum.

*An early shoe display. $25.00 – 75.00 a pair.* Courtesy of John and Mary Jo Purdum.

*The Self Weighing Shot Case, patented May 10, 1881. This is a very large cabinet with ten compartments for the various sizes of shot. $850.00 – 1,350.00.* Courtesy of John and Mary Jo Purdum.

*Three glass candy containers. Circa 1900. $40.00 – 95.00 each.*
Wilson Collection.

*Two glass candy containers. Circa 1900. $40.00 – 95.00 each.* Wilson Collection.

*A variety of glass candy jars, $40.00 – 95.00 each, and a German-silver showcase, $325.00 – 500.00.* Courtesy of El Dorado County Historical Society, Placerville, California.

*A beautiful one-unit German-silver showcase with impressive tiers at both ends, $1,500.00 – 2,750.00. Photo also shows a small etched-glass oak chewing gum case, $425.00 – 600.00.* Courtesy of John and Mary Jo Purdum.

*Adams Pepsin Tutti-Frutti Gum showcase. $425.00 – 650.00.* Courtesy of John and Mary Jo Purdum.

*A very scarce trade stimulator. It is encased in oak and offers the customer an opportunity to take a chance for 5¢ and perhaps win a prize. The customer will receive the 5¢ cigar he paid for and if the number "2" comes up, the customer will win a free cigar. $725.00 – 900.00.* Courtesy of John and Mary Jo Purdum.

*A cigar cutter, $22.00 – 35.00, and meat slicer, $35.00 – 55.00.* Courtesy of El Dorado County Historical Society, Placerville, California.

*A cheese cutter encased in oak. This cutter was used for years at the historic Smithflat Store in Smithflat, California. $275.00 – 350.00.* Courtesy of El Dorado County Historical Society, Placerville, California.

*Goff's "61" Braid Cabinet. $525.00 – 750.00.* Courtesy of
John and Mary Jo Purdum.

*The Best "Star" Braid wooden cabinet. $425.00 – 625.00.*
Courtesy of John and Mary Jo Purdum.

*Star Braid wooden cabinet with one drawer. $525.00 – 775.00.*
Courtesy of John and Mary Jo Purdum.

*Woolson Spice Company Fine Coffee floor bin,
$425.00 – 725.00. On top of the bin are two
early Blankes Mojav Coffee tins, $75.00 – 145.00
each.* Courtesy of John and Mary Jo Purdum.

*An unusual Red Pot Coffee bean dispenser. This attractive unit generally was positioned on a counter to draw quick attention. There is an opening at the bottom of the other side to dispense the coffee beans. $500.00 – 750.00.* Courtesy of El Dorado County Historical Society, Placerville, California.

*Ariston Mills Calumet Tea & Coffee Co. shelf caddy. Chicago, Illinois. $90.00 – 140.00.* Wilson Collection.

*Finest Family Tea shelf caddy. $85.00 – 140.00.* Wilson Collection.

*Large store tea caddy with double lithograph of a beautiful lady. This caddy is very ornate and stands 2 ft. high. $650.00 – 925.00.* Wilson Collection.

*A close-up of this outstanding container.*

*Large shelf caddy marked "Japan." Used for tea. Highly stenciled and has a lithographed portrait of a beautiful lady. Circa 1890. $350.00 – 475.00.* Courtesy of El Dorado County Historical Society, Placerville, California.

*Large tea caddy with two women pictured. $425.00 – 650.00.* Wilson Collection.

*Large green and gold Old Govt. Java shelf caddy. Circa 1890. $425.00 – 650.00.* Wilson Collection.

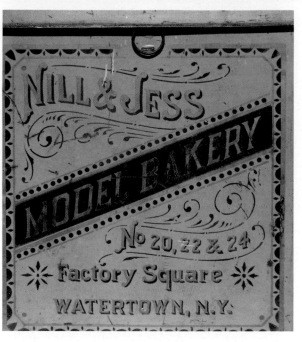

*Nill & Jess Model Bakery shelf caddy. Watertown, New York. $225.00 – 350.00.* Wilson Collection.

*Small spice shelf caddy with lithographed woman. Circa 1890. $175.00 –250.00.* Wilson Collection.

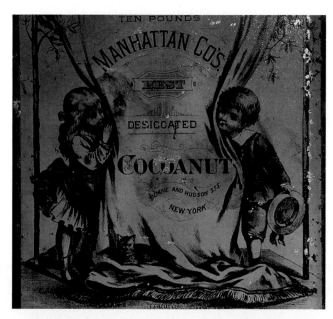

*Close-up detail of a Manhatten Co's. Cocoanut shelf caddy. The container held ten pounds and was made by the S.A. Ilsley & Co., New York. Circa 1879. $85.00 – 125.00.* Wilson Collection.

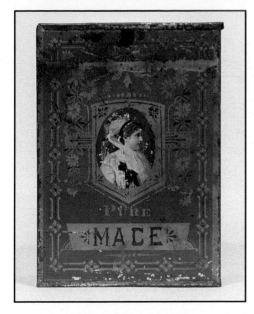

*A mace shelf caddy with lithographed portrait of a beautiful lady. $75.00 – 125.00.* Wilson Collection.

*Three shelf caddies for white pepper, cloves, and allspice. The Closset & Bevers Company. $60.00 – 100.00 each.* Courtesy of John and Mary Jo Purdum.

*An oak merchandiser. These are often referred to as "bean counters" or "grain counters." This one has the added feature of pull-out bins on the lower section. I have seen early wholesale store supply catalogs offering merchandisers to the general store trade and they were frequently used. $2,400.00 – 3,200.00. The counter contains a small Clark's O.N.T. Spool Cotton Thread Cabinet, $225.00 – 275.00, and a Potter's Embroidery Silk Cabinet, $225.00 – 275.00. Other store collectibles include a National Cash Register, $625.00 – 1,250.00; a cracker container, $45.00 – 60.00; a glass candy jar, $35.00 – 65.00; and a scale, $85.00 – 135.00.* Courtesy of John and Mary Jo Purdum.

*Clark's O.N.T. spool cabinet, George A. Clark, Sole Agent. Walnut. $950.00 – 2,250.00.* Courtesy of John and Mary Jo Purdum.

*Willimantic Soft Finish Spool Cotton cabinet. $850.00 – 1,500.00.* Courtesy of John and Mary Jo Purdum.

*Merrick's Six Cord Soft Finish spool cabinet. Patent date is July 20, 1897. The curved glass sections show thread and size as it is dialed by turning the handle at top. $825.00 – 1,250.00.* Courtesy of John and Mary Jo Purdum.

*Rit Cake or Flake dye cupboard. Lithographed tin with several wooden drawers in the back. Circa 1920. $225.00 – 375.00.* Wilson Collection.

*Rexall Household Dyes cabinet with mirror. $325.00 – 575.00.* Courtesy of John and Mary Jo Purdum.

*Pure Dye spool cabinet. 100 yards for 5¢. $325.00 – 475.00.* Courtesy of John and Mary Jo Purdum.

*Belding's Spool Silk cabinet. Oak. $625.00 – 825.00. Also, a small counter box for D. Mason & Co's Fine Laces, $65.00 – 85.00.* Courtesy of John and Mary Jo Purdum.

*J & P Coats Spool Cotton thread case. Oak. This unit was on a swivel base. Top-loaded with delivery through the bottom drawers. $625.00 – 900.00.* Courtesy of John and Mary Jo Purdum.

*R.J. Roberts "Parabola" Needles two-drawer wooden cabinet. $275.00 – 425.00. Standard Machine Needles one-drawer wooden case. $200.00 – 300.00.* Courtesy of John and Mary Jo Purdum.

*Crowley's Needles cabinet. Twelve drawers. $325.00 – 475.00.* Courtesy of John and Mary Jo Purdum.

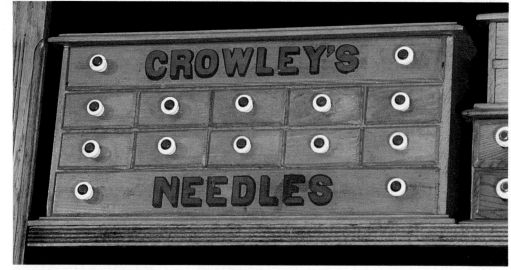

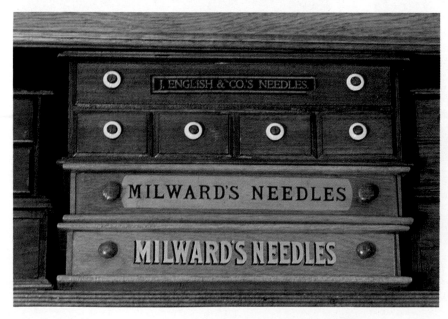

*Three needle cabinets. On the top is a J. English & Co.'s needle cabinet, $275.00 – 425.00. The other two are cabinets that contain Milward's needles, $250.00 – 350.00 each.* Courtesy of John and Mary Jo Purdum.

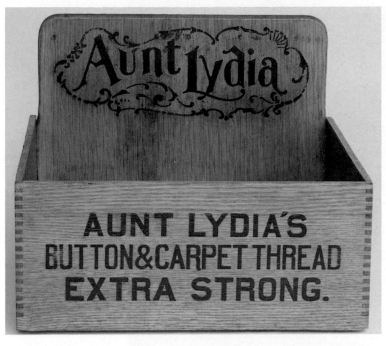

*Aunt Lydia's Button & Carpet Thread. Oak box. $75.00 – 100.00.*
Wilson Collection.

*A large 5-tier wooden ribbon cabinet that was almost always found in the dry goods section of the old general store. $750.00 – 1,250.00.* Courtesy of John and Mary Jo Purdum.

*The Clauss Shear Company, Fremont, Ohio. Etched-glass display case. $550.00 – 800.00.* Courtesy of John and Mary Jo Purdum.

*Ever Ready Dress Stay oak counter cabinet with etched glass. $175.00 – 250.00.* Wilson Collection.

*German-silver showcase with etched advertising. Hill's Cough Syrup, Peerless Worm Specific and Cobb's Podophyllin Pills. $625.00 – 950.00.* Courtesy of John and Mary Jo Purdum.

*Dr. Joseph Enk's Homeopathic Preparations cabinet. $650.00 – 900.00.* Courtesy of John and Mary Jo Purdum.

*Humphreys Remedies cabinet. $750.00 – 1,250.00.* Courtesy of John and Mary Jo Purdum.

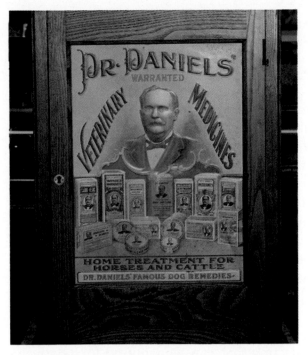

*Dr. Daniels Veterinary Medicines cabinet. Many of the products illustrated on the front of the cabinet are available to collectors. $1,250.00 – 2,600.00.* Courtesy of John and Mary Jo Purdum.

*Another Dr. Daniels Veterinary Medicines cabinet but this has a scarce embossed heavy paper insert on the front of the cabinet rather than the usual tin one. $850.00 – 1,750.00.* Courtesy of John and Mary Jo Purdum.

*Columbia Veterinary Remedies cabinet, The F. C. Sturtevant Company, Hartford, Connecticut. $750.00 – 1,350.00.* Courtesy of John and Mary Jo Purdum.

*Dr. Claris Veterinary Medicines cabinet. Oak. $450.00 – 700.00.* Courtesy of John and Mary Jo Purdum.

# Chapter Three
## TIN, WOODEN, & OTHER CONTAINERS

The year was 1968. I had left my home in California and was exuberant with thoughts of a vacation adventure and seeking out collectible tins and country store items. Two weeks to roam at will, see some great places and, hopefully, acquire some pieces for my collection. I had only $600.00 to finance the trip and make purchases but, at that time, it seemed more than adequate. I traveled through Nevada, Utah, Colorado, Kansas, Nebraska, and Missouri. I can still recall that trip as though it were yesterday. Union Leader and George Washington lunchbox tobacco tins for $2.50 to $5.00 each. An Ariston Mills Calumet Tea & Coffee store container found in Silverton, Colorado, for $7.50. A Tiger Tobacco store container for $8.00 in Missouri and a Sweet Burley Light Tobacco store container for $7.00. Those were truly exciting days to be a collector. Prices were very good and a huge variety of merchandise

seemed to be available. I chuckle now when I think about returning home from that trip with several great tin containers and just enough money for gasoline.

I feel it is every bit as exciting to be a collector today but, as always, things have changed somewhat over time. Recent auctions have brought some lofty prices for tin containers. Prices of over $100.00 at an advertising and country store show are not uncommon for a single tin. The collector today can be selective and seek out containers that are particularly appealing to him or her. There are still collectible tins that can be acquired for relatively modest amounts. Some collectors are only interested in "mint" or "near-mint" condition while others are very satisfied to find good representative examples. Looking for less than perfect or near-perfect tins can be much less frustrating and easier on the pocketbook. For

*Five containers left to right: Hewlett Bro.'s Co.'s Pure 3 Crown Spices tin caddy, $95.00 – 165.00; The Underwood Talmage Co. wooden candy box with lithographed label, Dayton, Ohio, $375.00 – 550.00; small and large containers of Fun To Wash Washing Powder, $12.00 – 25.00 each; a box of Fairbanks Gold Dust, $6.00 – 10.00.*
Courtesy of John and Mary Jo Purdum.

example, a particular tobacco tin in "mint" condition may bring $300.00 while its brother with some blemishes, small scratches, or general shelf wear may bring only $140.00 but still look great on the collector's display shelf. The decision is yours.

### Condition & Value

A number of factors can influence the value of a tin but most collectors would agree that condition is most important. The condition of a tin can range from "new" or "mint" condition to "poor" condition.

The "mint" or "almost mint" containers show little or no evidence of handling. The colors are very bright and the graphics are near perfect. There may be some very slight defects but nothing significant.

Most of the containers that are generally available fall into the category of "good" or "fair" condition. A tin in good condition may exhibit some faded color, nicks and scratches, or possibly even some small dents or rust. The graphics should remain clear with none of the lettering or other illustrations missing. Tins in

"fair" condition can be very collectible but may display significant shelf wear, fading, rust, or related conditions. It can be possible to improve the look of a tin container substantially through professional restoration. That subject will be discussed in a later chapter.

Tin containers in "poor" condition will naturally show substantial defects including paint that has completely faded, poor graphics, and advanced rust or other damage. Most serious collectors do not consider this category unless the particular tin happens to be very rare or possibly is a candidate for restoration. If the container is large and only has lettering with no subject or scene, there is a chance to do some worthwhile restoration.

Many tins contain the same graphics on the front and the rear of the container. Often, one of the illustrations is substantially damaged but the other illustration remains in very good condition. This condition will permit the collector to purchase the tin at a more favorable price. Once the tin is in your collection and on display, you simply turn the poor side to the rear and enjoy it!

*A small tin of Dr. David Roberts Gall Balm, $26.00 – 37.00; Dr. David Roberts Laxotone, $32.00 – 45.00.* Wilson Collection.

*Newton's Heave, Cough, Distemper and Indigestion Compound. The Newton Horse Remedy Co., Toledo, Ohio. $85.00 – 135.00.* Wilson Collection.

*AB Brand Coffee, Sacramento, California.*
*$36.00 – 55.00.* Wilson Collection.

*Dr. Johnson's Educator Crackers, $42.00 – 60.00.* Wilson Collection.

*Golden West glass, $18.00 –*
*25.00; and tin coffee containers,*
*$35.00 – 45.00.* Wilson Collection.

One last word about condition. A collector will usually pay more for a tin container in "mint" or "near-mint" condition than one in good condition. If appreciation is of great consideration to the collector, all things being equal, the "mint" or "near-mint" tin will generally increase in price at a rate significantly higher than the "good" condition tin. Of course, a lot of this will be affected by your original purchase price. If you paid too much, you may need to hang on to that particular tin for a period of time before you consider selling it.

Placing a value on a specific tin container is very difficult. There are no specific retail prices but there is a range of prices that containers are sold for. Rarity, condition, motivation of the seller and buyer, and other factors can all enter into a selling price. As you attend various antique shows and visit antique shops, this will be clearly demonstrated. I recall attending an advertising and country store auction in Ohio and observed an item sold for the high bid of $90.00. I felt that was probably a fair price. A few weeks later, I attended an antique show and found the same item for sale by a dealer for $225.00. I noted that it was the one at the auction. I had examined it closely since I intended to bid on it. How many hands did that item go through in a few weeks? Was it worth $225.00?

In my opinion, no way. I asked for the dealer's lowest price and the item was offered to me for $175.00.

The more knowledge you possess the more effective and satisfied you will be in making your purchases. Since there are no "list" prices for country store collectibles, one should become aware of the general range of prices. Purchasing from dealers and other sources you have confidence in is a good practice to follow.

*Best Value Coffee tin. The Weidemann Co., Cleveland, Ohio. $35.00 – 52.00.* Wilson Collection.

*Sherman Bros. & Co's. Orizaba Coffee tin, Chicago. $32.00 – 55.00.* Wilson Collection.

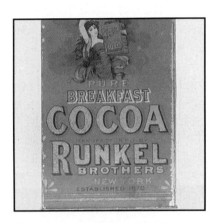

*Runkel Brothers Breakfast Cocoa. Runkel Brothers, New York. $25.00 – 40.00.* Wilson Collection.

*C. Maginn & Co. Crackers, Pittsburgh, Pennsylvania. $100.00 – 185.00.* Courtesy of John and Mary Jo Purdum.

*Guy Sayles Wholesale Grocer ginger caddy. Elmira, New York. $115.00 – 225.00.* Courtesy of John and Mary Jo Purdum.

## Why Old Tin Containers are in Such Demand

Many of the qualities that attracted customers of the old general store to tin containers also attract collectors. Tins were usually very colorful, with orange being a popular color. The graphics offered every theme imaginable and called for attention from the crowded shelves of the old store. To the collector, tins can offer a road to the past. Many have scenes depicting factories and buildings that no longer exist. There is always the possibility of making a rare discovery and adding to the knowledge about early tin containers. There is something very enjoyable about holding a small piece of history in your hand.

Additionally, it is virtually impossible to reproduce a lithographed tin container and capture the authentic old look and characteristic aging signs that these old containers have.

Designers created an incredible number and variety of distinctive designs and manufacturers had just about anything available to them. Beautiful women, rosy-cheeked children and robust babies were very popular themes. The old-time designers by virtue of their creative abilities contributed substantially to the continued preservation of tins. Without the wonderful graphics on the containers, many customers in the old days would not have been as much inclined to keep them. Many were used for storage of such things as pins and needles, coins, jewelry, and other personal items over the years.

Hunting for collectible tins can be a very enjoyable pastime. I'm still very excited to find a special tin for my collection. Many can be found for under $25.00 but if demand continues, prices will continue to rise. At this time, the demand appears to be very strong.

*Burns Spices cinnamon, Challenge Mills ginger, and Malaga cream tartar tins. $75.00 – 135.00 each.* Courtesy of John and Mary Jo Purdum.

*Schnull & Co. store caddy, Indianapolis, $120.00 – 185.00; Happy Home Brand store caddy, Packed For Rice Grocery Co., Scranton, Pennsylvania, $120.00 – 185.00; Pure Spice Black Pepper store caddy, The Widlar Co., Cleveland, Ohio, $95.00 – 145.00.* Courtesy of John and Mary Jo Purdum.

Waltham Watch Co., Waltham, Massachusetts, Main Springs tin container. $10.00 – 15.00. Wilson Collection.

Best Yet Coffee tin, Betterton Rupert Coffee Co., Ashland, Kentucky. $22.00 – 35.00. Wilson Collection.

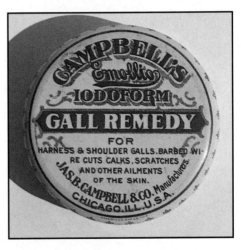

Tone Bros. Malabar and Lampong Black Pepper. Tone Brothers, Des Moines, Iowa. This is not an old tin but it does have nice graphics. $12.00 – 25.00. Wilson Collection.

Campbell's Iodoform Gall Remedy, Jas. B. Campbell & Co., Chicago. $10.00 – 15.00. Wilson Collection.

Betsy Ross Shoe Polish tin. The Black Cat Polish Co., Buffalo, New York. $14.00 – 22.00. Wilson Collection.

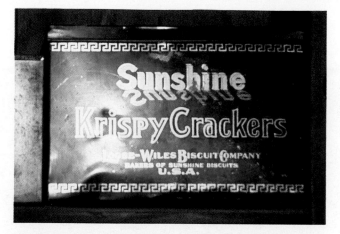

*Tin "Monarch Brand" ribbon spool. Edwards & Hancock, Chicago. $2.00 – 6.00.* Wilson Collection.

*Sunshine Krispy Crackers tin. $38.00 – 65.00.* Courtesy of El Dorado County Historical Society, Placerville, California.

*Electric Brand Golden Pumpkin label, Olney & Floyd, Westernville, Oneida County, New York. $2.50 – 5.00.* Wilson Collection.

*Seneca Canning Co. Pumpkin, Seneca, Michigan. Fruits of California pie fruit tin packed by T. S. Merchant, Healdsburg, Sonoma Co., California. $12.00 – 22.00 each.* Wilson Collection.

*Purity Teas, Coffees and Spices milk pail container. Decatur Extract Co., Decatur, Illinois. $160.00 – 240.00.* Courtesy of John and Mary Jo Purdum.

*F. H. Leggett & Co.'s Standard Spices. $135.00 – 225.00.* Courtesy of El Dorado County Historical Society, Placerville, California.

*Cream City Flour Bin & Sifter. $225.00 – 375.00.* Courtesy of El Dorado County Historical Society, Placerville, California.

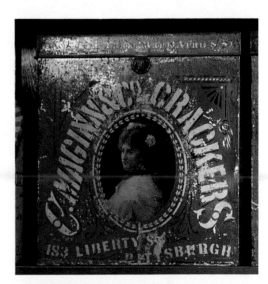

*Part of a set of C. Maginn & Co. Cracker caddies. $135.00 – 200.00 each.* Courtesy of John and Mary Jo Purdum.

*Additional C. Maginn & Co. Cracker caddies. $135.00 – 200.00 each.* Courtesy of John and Mary Jo Purdum.

*Top shelf: Caswell's Coffee, $25.00 – 40.00; Airway Coffee Bag, $6.00 – 9.00. Golden Robin Coffee, $45.00 – 75.00; JSB Coffee in milk pail container, $85.00 – 155.00; Dependable Coffee, $45.00 – 75.00. Bottom shelf: Four Edgemere Brand coffee tins, $55.00 – 80.00 each, Woolson Spice Co.* Courtesy of El Dorado County Historical Society, Placerville, California.

*Four large tea caddies. Ornate designs and illustrations. $325.00 – 550.00 each.* Courtesy of El Dorado County Historical Society, Placerville, California.

*Log Cabin syrup, $15.00 – 22.00; two containers of Imperial Granum Food, $25.00 – 37.00 each; Armour's Star Pure Lard pail, $15.00 – 27.00.* Courtesy of El Dorado County Historical Society, Placerville, California.

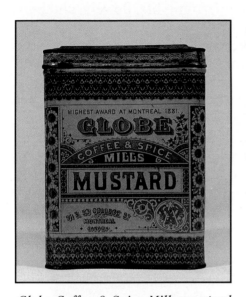

*Globe Coffee & Spice Mills mustard container. Globe Mills, Montreal, Canada. $55.00 – 90.00.* Wilson Collection.

*Hills Bros. Pure Spices shelf caddy, $55.00 – 85.00, and an Eddy & Eddy caddy illustrated with oak leaves and nuts and a quaint scene. This container would have held spices, $125.00 – 175.00.* Courtesy of El Dorado Historical Society, Placerville, California.

*A side photo of the Globe Mills mustard tin. Very nice graphics.* Wilson Collection.

*A nice display of peanut butter pails. Includes Jumbo Peanut Butter; Yankee Peanut Butter; Dayton Peanut Butter; Frontenag Peanut Butter; Sultana Peanut Butter and Red Seal Peanut Butter. $75.00 – 275.00 each.* Courtesy of John and Mary Jo Purdum.

## Wooden & Paper Containers

Wooden and paper containers are very popular. Many have striking illustrations on the outside and interior lids. On large wooden boxes such as cracker boxes and seed boxes, the outside label was exposed to rough treatment and the elements but the inner label was protected and often remains bright and colorful. It is truly remarkable that so many of the large wooden boxes and small paper boxes have survived over the years. Many were used as fire kindling and given to the tender mercies of children. Everything from Fairbanks Soap to Adams Chewing Gum was boxed in attractive containers.

Seed boxes are among the most brilliantly colored of the wooden boxes. Many have quaint scenes of farming life, flowers, children, or vegetables.

Wooden boxes are certainly a heritage of the old general store. They brought products such as Quaker Oats, Fels-Naptha soap, Peruvian Bitters, and G. H. Bent's Cold Water Crackers.

The smaller cardboard and paper containers that offered sewing thread, fancy soaps, candy, and an endless variety of other products are highly sought after by collectors. Many of them were not as durable as the larger wooden boxes so it is a real joy to find one in outstanding condition.

*Various brands of rolled oats paper boxes. $45.00 – 125.00 each.* Courtesy of John and Mary Jo Purdum.

*Additional rolled oats paper boxes. $45.00 – 125.00 each.* Courtesy of John and Mary Jo Purdum.

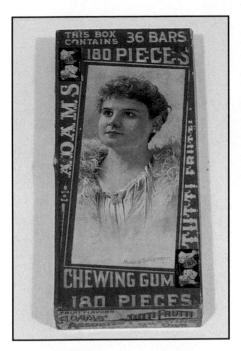

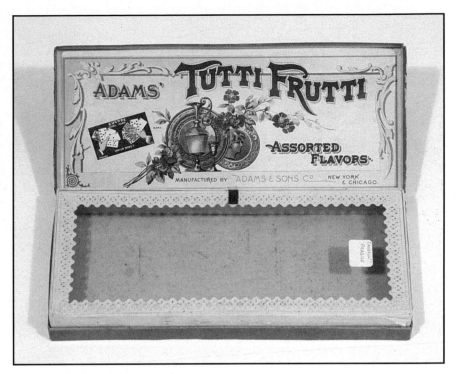

*Adams Tutti Frutti Chewing Gum box. Box held 180 pieces. $90.00 – 165.00.* Courtesy of Ron Schieber.

*Adams Tutti Frutti Assorted Flavors gum box for counter display. $75.00 – 150.00.* Courtesy of Ron Schieber.

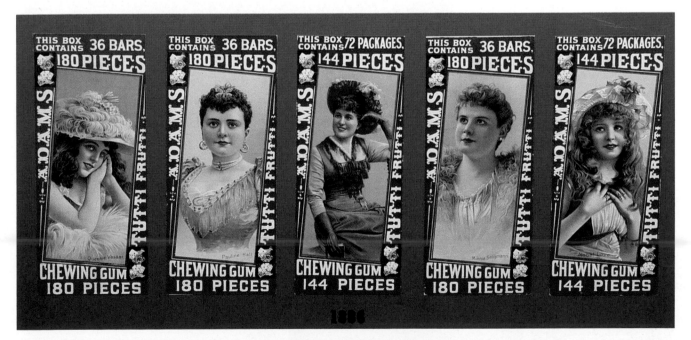

*A collection of labels for the tops of Adams Tutti Frutti Gum boxes. These labels were never used and remain a testimonial to the magic of early-day lithography. $100.00 – 175.00 each.* Courtesy of Ron Schieber.

*King Bee Coffee bin; The C. F. Ware Coffee Company bin, Dayton, Ohio. $425.00 – 650.00.* Courtesy of John and Mary Jo Purdum.

*Two floor coffee bins of wood. On the left is "Magic Blend" from the James Hargan Co. of Madison, Indiana, $375.00 – 500.00. The box on the right is from Dayton Spice Mills and contained roasted coffee, $450.00 – 700.00.* Courtesy of John and Mary Jo Purdum.

*Shelf caddies for Blanke's India Tea, $225.00 – 350.00; and Phelps Krag & Co's. Blue Cross Coffee, $225.00 – 300.00.* Courtesy of John and Mary Jo Purdum.

Golden Rio Coffee bin. Griffin & Hoxie, Acme Mills, Utica, New York. $425.00 – 650.00. Courtesy of El Dorado County Historical Society, Placerville, California.

*Toledo Spice Company German Coffee floor bin. $425.00 – 650.00.* Courtesy of John and Mary Jo Purdum.

*Dover Egg Beater cardboard container. The box holds 60 egg beaters. Pat. Feb. 9, 1904. $22.00 – 38.00.* Courtesy of John and Mary Jo Purdum.

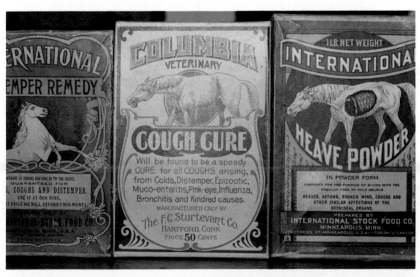

*International Distemper Remedy box, International Stock Food Co.; Minneapolis, Minnesota; Columbia Veterinary Cough Cure box, The F. C. Sturtevant Co., Hartford, Connecticut; International Heave Powder box; International Stock Food Co., Minneapolis, Minnesota. $52.00 – 75.00 each.* Wilson Collection.

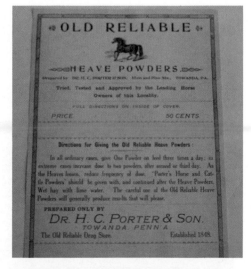

*Old Reliable Heave Powders label. Dr. H. C. Porter & Son, Towanda, Pennsylvania. $3.00 – 6.00.* Wilson Collection.

*Heinz's shipping crate for three dozen Baked Beans with Tomato Sauce. J.J. Heinz Co., Pittsburgh. Side panel advertises Heinz's India Relish. $55.00 – 85.00.* Courtesy of Twinsburg Historical Society.

*The end label with graphics of the large wooden Heinz's Baked Beans box.*

*W. J. Sands & Sons Biscuits & Crackers. Wooden shipping box. Erie Steam Bakery, Erie, Pennsylvania. $125.00 – 200.00.* Courtesy of Twinsburg Historical Society.

*Vellastic Underwear box. $37.00 – 55.00.* Courtesy of John and Mary Jo Purdum.

*Buckeye Sash Holder. Paper box. Buckeye Manufacturing Company, Central City, Nebraska. $10.00 – 17.00.* Wilson Collection.

*Our Leader suspenders cardboard box. $52.00 – 85.00.* Wilson Collection.

*Colburn's Bag Blue For Laundry Use. Wooden box with lithographed label. $225.00 – 375.00.* Courtesy of John and Mary Jo Purdum.

*Grandpa's Wonder Soap wooden shipping box. The Beaver Soap Co., Dayton, Ohio. $125.00 – 175.00.* Courtesy of John and Mary Jo Purdum.

*Label from a large box of Queen Beauty Toilet Soap. Dr. B. Lynas & Son, Logansport, Indiana. $4.00 – 8.00.* Wilson Collection.

*Proctor & Gamble Lenox Soap, Cincinnati, Ohio. $95.00 – 175.00.* Courtesy of John and Mary Jo Purdum.

*Just Fits The Hand Lenox Soap wooden packing box. $95.00 – 175.00. Note: This box brought only $35.00 at an auction April 3, 1996, evidence that there are still bargains out there!* Courtesy of John and Mary Jo Purdum.

*Celluloid box with pretty girl. Used for combs, brushes, and other personal items. $65.00 – 85.00.* Wilson Collection.

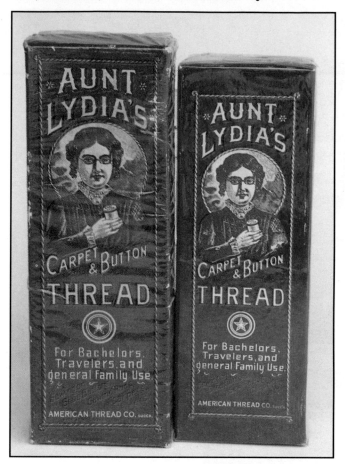

*Aunt Lydia's Carpet & Button Thread boxes. American Thread Co., Willimantic, Connecticut. $15.00 – 24.00 each.* Wilson Collection.

*Clark's O.N.T. Thread box. $8.00 – 12.00.* Wilson Collection.

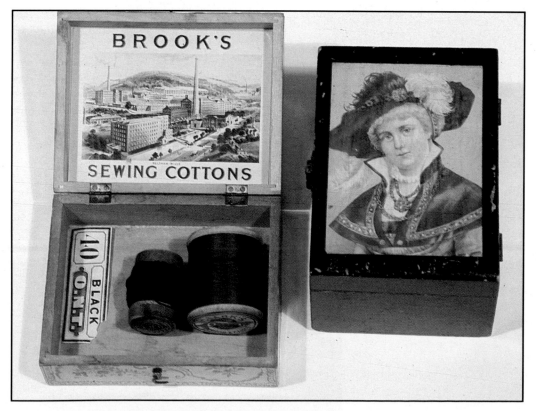

*Containers for Brooks Sewing Cottons & soap. $27.00 – 40.00.* Courtesy of Ron Schieber.

*A Brooks Spool Cotton tin container, a Brooks Spool Cotton wooden container; a J. & P. Coats Spool Cotton & Crochet wooden box. $25.00 – 50.00 each.* Courtesy of Ron Schieber.

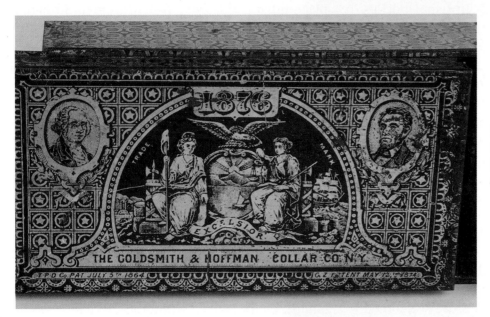

*The Goldsmith & Hoffman Collar Co. tin, New York. The lid slides back to expose the contents. $45.00 – 75.00.* Wilson Collection.

*Berry Brothers Celebrated Varnishes shipping box, $45.00 – 70.00; Kelly's Grocery box, $18.00 – 35.00.* Courtesy of El Dorado County Historical Society, Placerville, California.

# Chapter Four
## ❖ THE BIG PROFIT SHELF: ❖
## MIRACLES BY THE BOTTLE
### Patent Medicines, Remedies, Elixirs, & Other Personal Needs

DR. WILSON'S RESTORATIVE REMEDIES, HALL'S CATARRH CURE, DR. JOHN BULL'S VEGETABLE WORM DESTROYER, DR. RAPHAEL'S GALVANIC LOVE POWDERS, AYERS CHERRY PECTORAL, PERUVIAN BITTERS, BALM OF CHILDHOOD, SLOAN'S LINIMENT, HOLLOWAY'S WORM CONFECTIONS, DR. SIM'S ARSENIC COMPLEXION WAFERS, DRAKE'S PLANTATION BITTERS, KICKAPOO INDIAN COUGH CURE, PINK PILLS FOR PALE PEOPLE...

The amazing variety of patent medicines, remedies, elixirs and nostrums available to the general store was seemingly unending. Store shelves were filled with unusual bottles with fancy labels and incredible claims. Customers looked to the storekeeper to stock favorite brands. It was a customer's delight because the makers of the "medicines" offered diagnosis and prescription without ever examining the patient. The offerings ran the gamut from occasionally helpful to worthless. Beyond that, the cure-alls could result in blindness, paralysis, and even death.

There were 3,000 medicine makers marketing more than 10,000 brand names or labels. Sales reached the staggering level of about 300 million bottles or containers during the glory years. Colonel Hostetter of Hostetter's Bitters accumulated a fortune estimated at $18,000,000! The local general store welcomed the enthusiastic demand. The large apothecary section in most stores was testimonial to the incredible variety available for sale, the demand, and the handsome profits to be made.

During the golden years of the American general store, sparse populations and an isolated lifestyle served to create a high degree of self-sufficiency. Selection of treatment was the order of the day. Perhaps the very allure of the remedies was the mystique. A rugged rural way of life caused many people to seek relief from a variety of aches and pains. Chills, ulcers, rheumatism, colic, snakebites, and lame backs were just a few. Scarcity of qualified doctors coupled with a general distrust of the medical profession caused an individual to seek a cheap, quick, and painless road to good health. Some historians feel that the medical practices in place during the Civil War prompted an avoidance of physicians by numbers of people for many years. The harsh and often fatal treatment that was commonplace on the battlefield resulted in lingering fears. "Granny" remedies and magic cure-alls were substituted for proper medical care in many cases. Cure-it-by-the-bottle was accepted as a genuine form of treatment.

Advertising was the key to generating demand. The walls of general stores, barns, trees, or any handy place helped keep the remedy in the public eye and create a large demand. Nostrum literature was piled high on the counters of country stores. The ad writers of the day had free license to do anything to create demand and outlandish claims were commonplace. There was an alliance between the medicine-makers, newspapers, and popular magazines. The various publications made a great deal of money from the advertisements and asked no questions. The farmer's almanac had grown in popularity from Colonial times and became a great place for quackery advertising along with information on weather cycles, planting times, and other interesting tidbits. About November of every year, the new supply of almanacs arrived at the general store and were promptly placed on the counter for quick distribution. They were, of course, free of charge and eagerly grabbed up — one to a family. Trade cards came with medicines or were sent in return for a label from the

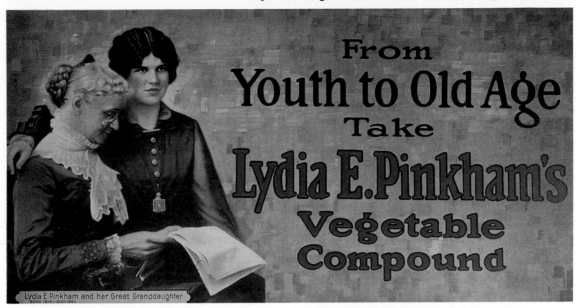

Store advertisement for Lydia E. Pinkham's Vegetable Compound. The public was so captivated by Lydia Pinkham that many continued to write personal letters to her long after Lydia's death. $135.00 – 225.00. Wilson Collection.

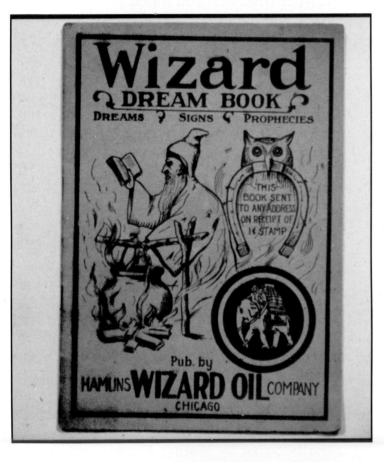

Wizard Dream Book which offers dream analysis, signs, and prophecies. Hamlins Wizard Oil Co., Chicago. $12.00 – 24.00. Wilson Collection.

Taylor's Improved Condition Powders! A paper sign with large lettering to call to customers in need. $18.00 – 25.00. Wilson Collection.

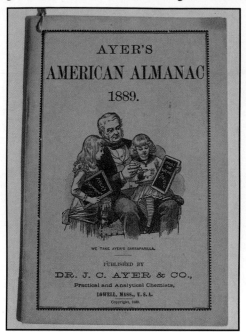

*Ayer's American Almanac for 1889. Dr. J. C. Ayer & Co., Lowell, Massachusetts. These almanacs and similar examples were passed out by the millions to promote the products. $7.00 – 12.00.*
Wilson Collection.

package. Favored customers were given special almanacs like the Hamlin's Wizard Oil Almanac which offered dream interpretation. Most of the almanacs were loaded with pages and pages of product advertising and testimonials. Merchants also had brightly lithographed calendars, trade cards, posters, and other items to give out to anxious hands. Anything readable and free was greatly appreciated. Many times, the store's name was prominently placed on the advertising item.

With all of the advertising taking place, it is not surprising that the crossroads store stocked an impressive variety of medicines to bring comfort to man or beast. Companies spent a substantial amount of profit to continue their advertising campaigns. In 1905 a leading drug trade journal listed the names of over 28,000 brands.

The general store's drug shelves became a place of both physical and spiritual comfort for the customers. Something always seemed to be available that offered just the relief being sought. The country store proprietor was often the source of a recommendation for the appropriate medicine. The storekeeper reaped the benefits of an enormous markup. Medicines that were sold to the general store for $3.00 a

dozen would be sold at a retail price of $1.00 a bottle. Cure-alls would also be sold to the store trade with no price on the bottle or container. This would permit a sale price of whatever the proprietor felt proper. Medicine companies and their sales forces often gave the storekeeper free samples to cultivate an interest in carrying their product. These giveaways were then sold to customers at a clear profit. No wonder the shelves were well-stocked with a huge selection of remedies.

There was virtually no control over the medicine industry and manufacturers would "brew" anything that resulted from their enterprise and some sort of basic formula. Greed was a strong motivator. At times, a manufacturer would develop one concoction and in turn sell it to distributors who would place their own name and brands on them.

The contents of the "medicines" were left to the imagination of the manufacturer. Some sincerely attempted to market products that were helpful and based on proven herb or Indian cures. Some contained bark, leaves, vegetables, roots and berries, and more often, the "cures" contained a substantial volume of alcohol. The alcoholic content of Hostetter's Celebrated Stomach Bitters, for example, was 44% by volume. Parker's Tonic had 41%. Those who had forsaken alcohol felt the medicinal value of bitters and "spring tonics" was truly worthwhile. Many remedies included addictive narcotics which were plentiful, cheap, and legal. Strychnine was used in the tonics to give them a genuine "belt." Morphine or other opium derivatives served as a base for pain killers. Soothing syrups for infants contained heavy doses of morphine. Other nostrums contained kerosene and camphor. Temporary "relief" from an affliction was the reward of a patent medicine, but the problem lingered on or was eventually cured by Mother Nature, not by the quack medicine. Bottles piled up behind barns and other places.

The label made outrageous claims. One product claimed to serve as a cure for 30 different afflictions! Many were sold with directions stating the contents to be appropriate for man or beast. Sloan's Liniment is a good example. The label on the bottle declares that it kills pain. The directions for man state the remedy is

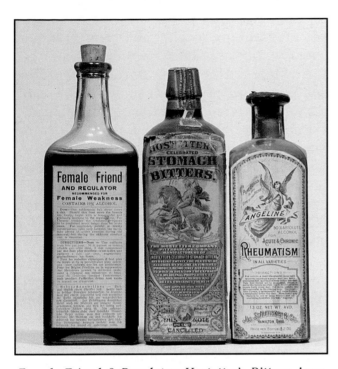

*Female Friend & Regulator; Hostetter's Bitters; Angeline For Acute & Chronic Rheumatism, 30% alcohol, Jos. Schumaker & Co., Hamilton, Ohio. $42.00 – 95.00 each.* Courtesy of Bumpas Emporium.

*The back page of* Daring Donald McKay or The Last War Trail of the Modocs. *It appears the nostrum will cure just about any affliction!* Wilson Collection.

*"Snake Oil" Booklet. Additional information about the virtues of Modoc Oil. $25.00 – 35.00.* Wilson Collection.

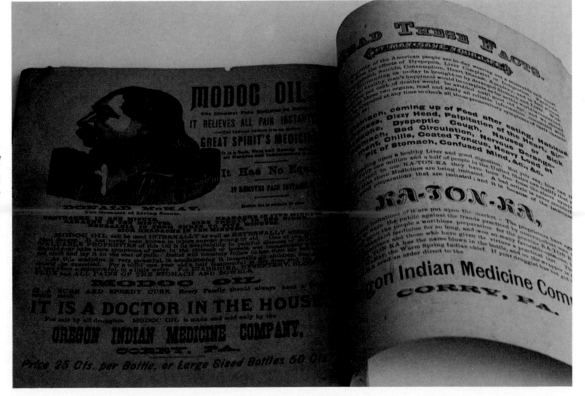

effective for rheumatism, toothache, headache, sore throat, cramp, colic, pleurisy and sciatica, among others. The directions on the same label proclaim that there are numerous benefits for horses. Cockle joints, spavin, thrush or canker, wind puffs and kicks can be treated and cured by the contents of the bottle. Due to the kerosene or alcohol content of the product, a caveat was often included on the label cautioning the user to keep the contents from fire or flame. All of this for 50 cents!

Two of the major afflictions of the nineteenth and early twentieth century were known as catarrh and ague. Catarrh was a phlegm in the back of the throat and ague was like flu, with fevers and chills. Injury was commonplace and a variety of sicknesses plagued the populace of the time. Poor diet, hard work and excessive exposure to the elements took their toll. The settlement of the Old West added illness and hardship to the daily lives of pioneers.

Painless cures were in fashion. The person in need had strong interest in the general store stock of cures. It was a challenge to select just the right pills, ointments, liniments, lozenges, or elixirs to cure everything from dropsy to St. Vitus's dance. Do-it-yourself medications were sought after. Calling the doctor could be expensive, time-consuming, and painful. Many people sought the patent panacea which caused proper treatment to be delayed. There was a significant shortage of qualified physicians and medical service was perceived by many to be inferior. Often, the doctor was called when the individual was beyond help. New "medicines" were promoted to cure alcohol and drug addiction caused by consumption of favorite remedies.

Although the term *patent medicine* sounded impressive, it was simply a trade name that was registered in Washington as the name of a commercial property. Registered trade names were good for eternity and the medicine-makers were very happy about that. The Pure Food and Drug Act of 1906 did not immediately eliminate the evils of quackery but did slow the process down. The endless flow of worthless cure-alls was being left in the past.

The general store's drug shelves also offered cough drops and related items, fancy perfumes, vaporizers, and other personal needs. The collector can seek out a bountiful array of items from the age of patent medicines — beautiful embossed bottles with quaint labels and striking graphics, wooden shipping boxes, trade cards, almanacs, posters, broadsides, and calendars, to name a few. Good hunting!

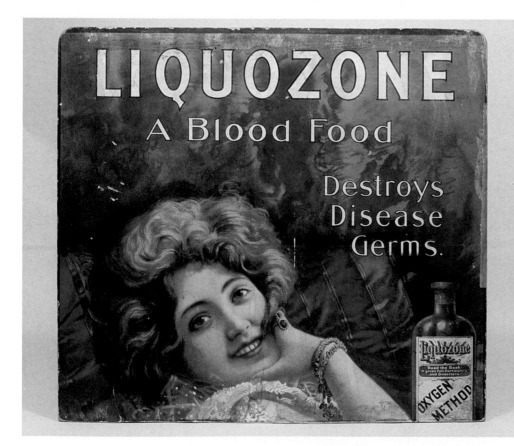

*Liquozone, A Blood Food. Claims to destroy disease germs. This was used as a stand-up counter ad. Liquozone had fallen on bad times and was just about out of business when an outstanding advertising copywriter came to the rescue. Claude Hopkins believed the product had saved his daughter's life and began to write glowing testimonies and effective ads. Before long, Liquozone became a great success throughout the world. $125.00 – 175.00.* Wilson Collection.

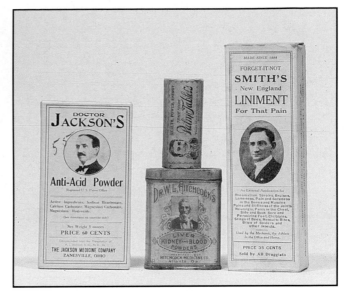

Hoff's Liniment with the major ingredients being ammonia, camphor, and turpentine. Goodrich-Gamble Co., St. Paul, Minnesota; Kalamazoo Celery, Blood & Nerve Tonic, Celery Medicine Co., Kalamazoo, Michigan; a larger size of Hoff's Liniment. It was priced at $1.00 and the smaller size was 65¢. $25.00 – 55.00 each. Courtesy of Bumpas Emporium.

Dr. Jackson's Anti-Acid Powder, The Jackson Medicine Company, Zanesville, Ohio; a small blue container of Health Tablets for Health, Power, and Energy; Dr. W. L. Hitchcock's Liver, Kidney and Blood Powders, Hitchcock Medicine Co., Atlanta, Georgia; Smith's New England Liniment For That Pain, made since 1884 and priced at 35¢. $22.00 – 50.00 each. Courtesy of Bumpas Emporium.

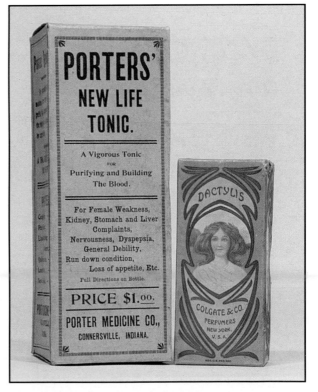

Var-Ne-Sis For Rheumatism, made in Lynn, Massachusetts; Smith's Liniment; Haddad's Stomach Elixir. Promoted as an herb tonic and produced by the Haddad Medical Co., Toledo, Ohio. $25.00 – 70.00 each. Courtesy of Bumpas Emporium.

Porters' New Life Tonic for purifying and building the blood. Porter Medicine Co., Connersville, Indiana; Dactylis Perfume box, Colgate & Co. Perfumers, New York. $8.00 – 15.00 each. Wilson Collection.

*Robert J. Pierce's Empress Brand Pennyroyal Tablets to cure suppression of the menstrual function. Priced at $2.00 and manufactured in Mount Vernon, New York. $55.00 – 75.00.* Wilson Collection.

*Pierce's Memorandum Account Book. Designed for farmers and mechanics and available free of charge. Numerous pages in the book were heavily devoted to pushing the company's products. $8.00 – 12.00.* Wilson Collection.

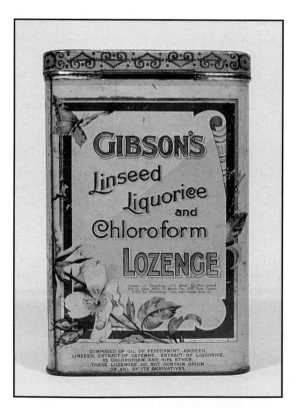

*Gibson's Linseed, Liquorice and Chloroform Lozenge tin container. $65.00 – 110.00.* Wilson Collection.

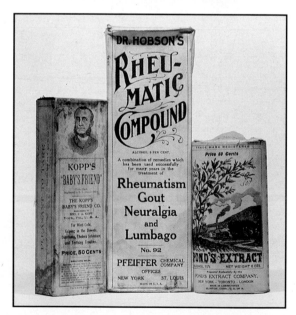

*Kopp's "Baby's Friend," The Kopp's Baby's Friend Co., York, Pennsylvania; Dr. Hobson's Rheumatic Compound, Pfeiffer Chemical Co., New York & St. Louis; Pond's Extract. $35.00 – 55.00 each.* Courtesy of Bumpas Emporium.

*A small tin of Mountain Rose Herbaline. Manufactured by Springsteen Medicine Co., Cleveland, Ohio, and was highly priced at $4.00. $10.00 – 15.00.* Wilson Collection.

*DeWitt's Syrup of Figs with Pepsin and Senna for Constipation, E. C. DeWitt & Co., Chicago; Trommer Diastasic Extract of Malt, The Trommer Co., Fremont, Ohio; a bottle of 500 tablets containing gonorrhea medication, The Upjohn Pill & Granule Co., Kalamazoo, Michigan. $28.00 – 75.00 each.* Courtesy of Bumpas Emporium.

*Hollister's Rocky Mountain Tea Nuggets, Hollister Drug Co., Madison, Wisconsin. $12.00 – 20.00.* Wilson Collection.

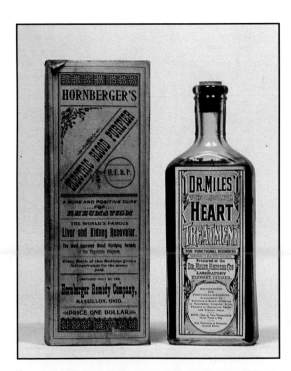

*Merchants Gargling Oil and Liniment For Man or Beast; sold since 1833. The extremely popular Hostetters Celebrated Stomach Bitters. This product appeared on the shelves of countless general stores and the very high alcohol content had much to do with the success of the product. Manufactured in Pittsburgh, Pennsylvania. Another popular product of the day was Dr. John Bull's Cough Syrup. Produced by the A. C. Meyer & Co. of Baltimore. $45.00 – 95.00 each.* Courtesy of Bumpas Emporium.

*Hornberger's Electric Blood Purifier: The World's Famous Liver and Kidney Renovator. Manufactured by the Hornberger Remedy Co., Massillon, Ohio, and priced at $1.00; Dr. Miles' Heart Treatment, Dr. Miles Medical Co., Elkhart, Indiana. $32.00 – 75.00 each.* Courtesy of Bumpas Emporium.

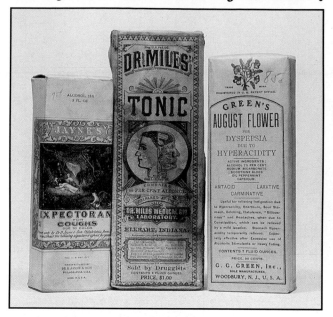

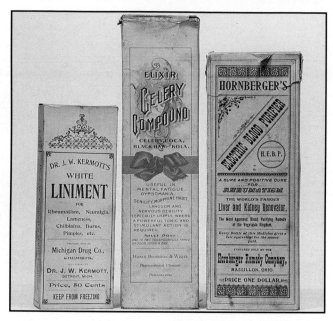

*Jayne's Expectorant For Coughs. Produced by Dr. Jayne & Son, Philadelphia; the box for Dr. Miles' Tonic; Green's August Flower For Dyspepsia. G. G. Green, Woodbury, New Jersey. $35.00 – 85.00 each.* Courtesy of Bumpas Emporium.

*Elixir Celery Compound, advertised as a powerful tonic and stimulant. $15.00 – 65.00; Dr. J. W. Kermott's White Liniment, Detroit. $15.00 – 65.00; Hornberger's Electric Blood Purifier: The World's Famous Liver and Kidney Renovator. $30.00 – 75.00.* Courtesy of Bumpas Emporium.

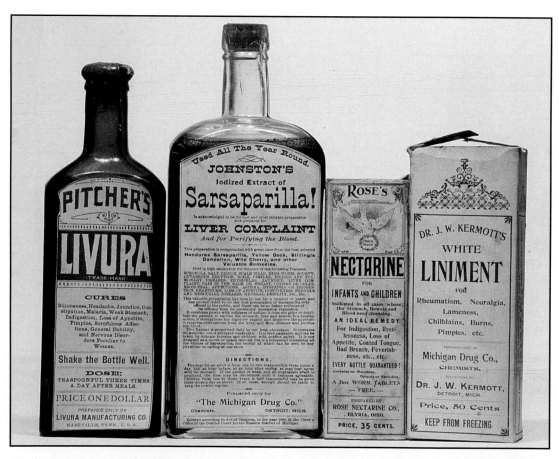

*Pitcher's Livura. Livura Manufacturing Co., Nashville, Tennessee; Johnston's Sarsaparilla For Liver Complaints and other problems. The Michigan Drug Co., Detroit; Rose's Nectarine For Infants & Children, Rose Nectarine Co., Elyia, Ohio; Dr. J. W. Kermott's White Liniment, Detroit. $24.00 – 75.00 each.* Courtesy of Bumpas Emporium.

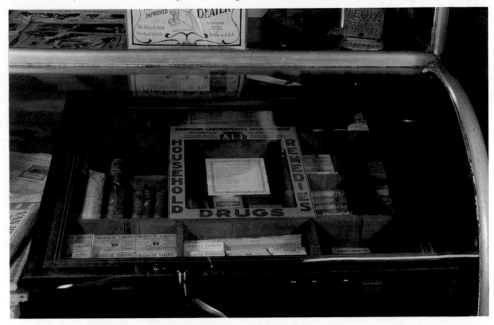

*Household Remedies & Drugs displayed in the original case. American Laboratories, Inc., Richmond, Virginia. $425.00 – 675.00.* Courtesy of John and Mary Jo Purdum.

*A variety of compounds and remedies. The green Parke, Davis & Co. tins contain such things as yellow dock root, wormwood and other herbs, leaves, flowers, barks, and roots. $40.00 – 65.00. The die-cut advertising sign with the elderly couple is for Ayer's Sarsaparilla. $140.00 – 225.00.* Courtesy of El Dorado County Historical Society, Placerville, California.

*Himrod's Asthma Powder for Asthma, Hay Fever, Nasal Catarrh and Ordinary Colds; Sloan's Liniment with separate directions for man and beast; Anisette Superfine liqueur; Watkins' Gen-De-Can-Dra For The Blood, 16% alcohol, "No Opium or Mineral Poisons"; Dr. J. D. Kellogg's Asthma Remedy, Northrop & Lyman Co., Inc., Buffalo, New York. $38.00 – 90.00 each.* Wilson Collection.

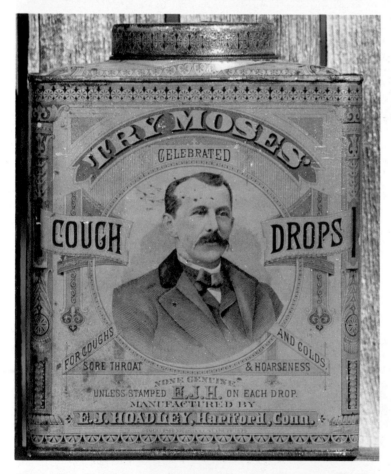

*Dr. Lynas' Vegetable Marvel Soap. $3.00 – 6.00.* Wilson Collection.

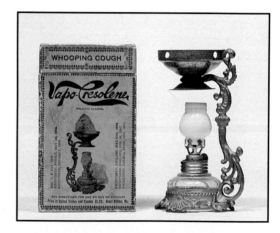

*Moses Cough Drops container manufactured by E. J. Hoadley, Hartford, Connecticut. This early tin is noted for its outstanding graphics. $200.00 – 375.00.* Wilson Collection.

*Vapo-Cresolene Lamp For Whooping Cough. $125.00 – 200.00.* Courtesy of Bumpas Emporium.

*Four bars of Queen Beauty Toilet Soap. Dr. J. B. Lynas & Son, Logansport, Indiana. $7.50 – 12.00 each.* Wilson Collection.

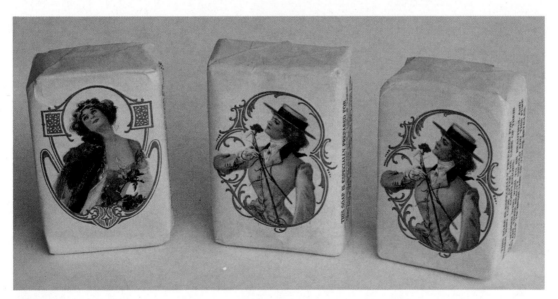

*Some additional beauties of the day captured on the front of Dr. J. B. Lynas & Son's Soaps. $7.50 – 12.00 each.* Wilson Collection.

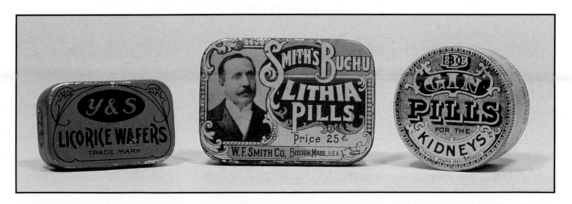

*Y & S Licorice Wafers, $7.00 – 15.00; Smith's Buchu Lithia Pills for Rheumatism and all diseases of the kidneys, blood, and urinary organs. Also good for Gout, Diabetes, Lumbago, Nervous Debility, and many others. W. F. Smith Co., Boston, $28.00 – 45.00; Gin Pills For The Kidneys, National Drug & Chemical Co. of Canada, $20.00 – 35.00.* Wilson Collection.

*Sykes Comfort Powder; Nyal Hirsutone For The Hair; Farr's Grey Hair Restorer. The Brookline Chemical Co., Boston; La-Mar Reducing Soap. Promises to wash away fat and years of age. La-Mar Laboratories, Cleveland, Ohio; Sanitol Liquid Shampoo, St. Louis. $22.00 – 65.00 each.* Courtesy of Bumpas Emporium.

*Dactylis Toilet Water, Colgate & Co., New York; Hairwealth Real Eau de Quinine; Youth Craft For The Hair & Scalp and Dandruff & Itching Scalp. Youth Craft Co., Chicago; Sozodont Powder For The Teeth; DeWitt's Toilet Cream. $30.00 – 70.00 each.* Courtesy of Bumpas Emporium.

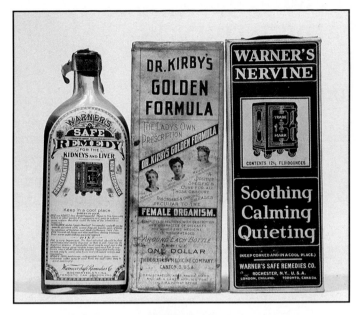

*Warner's Safe Remedy For The Kidneys And Liver, Warner's Safe Remedy Co., Rochester, New York; Dr. Kirby's Golden Formula, The Lady's Own Prescription. The Dr. Kirby Medicine Co., Canton, Ohio; Warner's Nervine, Warner's Safe Remedy Co., Rochester, New York. $45.00 – 65.00 each.* Courtesy of Bumpas Emporium.

*Father John's Medicine, touted to make flesh and maintain strength. Carleton & Hovey Co., Lowell, Massachusetts; Vix-Um for Asthma, Bronchitis, Colds, and Constipation. J. H. Kessler Laboratories, Cleveland, Ohio; Wheeler's Nerve Vitalixer. The J. C. Brant Co., Albion, Michigan. $22.00 – 55.00 each.* Courtesy of Bumpas Emporium.

*Hospital Carbolic Soap, $12.00 – 22.00; Women's Lakeside Chamois Vest To Prevent All Lung And Chest Troubles, $35.00 – 50.00.* Courtesy of Bumpas Emporium.

*John's Vegetable Oil Compound; DeWitt's Fruity Syrup; Dr. C. M. Simson's Nerve Compound; Dr. Bull's Cough Syrup. $25.00 – 55.00 each.* Courtesy of Bumpas Emporium.

# Chapter Five
## ❖OLD STORE ADVERTISING❖
### Advertising Giveaways
### & Auction Posters

As a growing volume of merchandise was made available to country merchants across America, an explosion of advertising accompanied it. Goods were promoted by everything from creative and colorful posters for the walls of the general store to miniature chromolithographics that became known as trade cards for giveaway to customers.

Early American advertisers were very familiar with the value of visual aids in pushing the product. Illustrators had a particular fondness for depicting children, beautiful women, utopian farm scenes, and animals in their advertisements. As brands and competition increased, the old country store reaped the benefit of a wide variety of advertising. The patent medicine companies provided free calendars and trade cards to be handed out to preferred customers. Everything was cheerfully accepted by the general store owner who enjoyed receiving free things from his suppliers and passing them along to customers.

The drummers who visited the store merchant were happy to be able to offer free advertising material as an incentive to sell merchandise. Holiday cards, pocket mirrors, pin back buttons, and other novelty items were abundant.

Of all the methods used, nothing had more popularity than trade cards. Virtually every product from shoes to sewing machines utilized this medium. They were handed out over the counter in general stores by the thousands upon thousands. Customers cherished them and frequently created special albums for them.

The 1800's through the early 1900's were the peak years and the quality and variety produced was truly amazing. They were particularly plentiful during the Christmas season to promote individual stores and specific merchandise. Woolson Spice Company was very

*Howard The Original and The Only Dustless-Duster. Large advertising store poster. $750.00 – 1,000.00.* Courtesy of Ron Schieber.

prolific, for example. Their cards remain as some of the most attractive.

Many cards were all-purpose stock types printed with general subjects or scenes and sold wholesale to a multitude of different companies. Often, the cards were then overprinted to advertise a specific general store.

Trade cards are generally the size of today's playing cards but there were a number of exceptions. Die-cut cards were also offered that were cut in the shape of the product they advertised. This chapter contains an illustration of such a card that is in the shape of a lady's shoe. Most cards had a full-color picture on one side with perhaps the name of the product and the local merchant's name. Some even had a short sales pitch. The other side of the card contained the lengthy sales pitch and other declarations.

By the turn of the century, some of the enthusiasm and interest for the cards was declining. A new sensation called the picture post card had been introduced and more emphasis was being placed on advertising in national magazines.

The celluloid-backed pocket mirror was another favorite with customers. Most pocket mirrors were very colorful and touted everything from coffee to stoves. There have been reproductions of pocket mirrors but the originals are rather easy to spot. Most authentic mirrors can be identified by locating the name of the maker which is usually imprinted on the edge of the mirror. Celluloid is uniform in appearance where it meets the mirror and the plastic used for reproductions is often not. If you see a notice on the celluloid portion of the mirror offering a duplicate for a few cents in postage, that is another clear sign of authenticity. Celluloid novelties were also offered in matchsafes, pin holders and paperweights, all with prominent advertising.

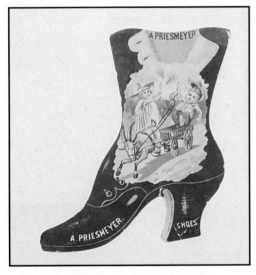

*Die-cut advertising card. A. Priesmeyer Ladies' Shoes and Young America School Shoes. Nothing cheap or shoddy. $6.00 – 12.00.* Wilson Collection.

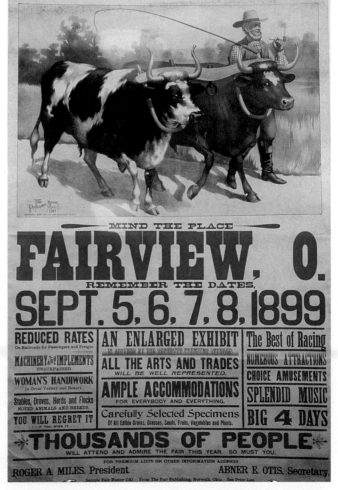

*Fairview, Ohio, Country Fair poster. $650.00 – 850.00.* Courtesy of Ron Schieber.

*White King Granulated Soap. Advertising giveaway. $12.00 – 25.00.* Courtesy of Ron Schieber.

The pinback button was also favored by customers of the general store. These small buttons advertised a host of products and were particularly looked forward to at Christmas when Santa Claus became the featured subject.

Farm auctions were much more frequent in early days. Death, bankruptcy, disillusionment, or simply a desire to move on would bring about an auction. It was necessary to get the word out to as many people as possible and there was no single place as frequently visited by the surrounding populace as the old general store. Notices of the forthcoming auction were often posted at the crossroads store. The auction posters typically had woodcuts of household goods and farming equipment of the day as well as livestock. Many were very elaborate and

have generally been overlooked as a worthwhile collectible from the days of the early stores. Most were printed on heavy paper using standard woodcuts but I have seen some on fabric and some with fascinating illustrations. They are very collectible and can be found. I recall talking with a gentleman in 1970 who was 96 at that time and had been raised in Missouri. He told me that auction notices were always posted at the store he patronized and he remembered them vividly.

Old store advertising items come in all shapes and sizes and degrees of rarity. Just when you feel that you have seen everything, a new discovery is made. I wish you good fortune in your search and the added thrill of finding something that has been in storage for years.

*AIC High Grade Coffees. Advertising poster on heavy paper. $75.00 – 125.00.* Courtesy of John and Mary Jo Purdum.

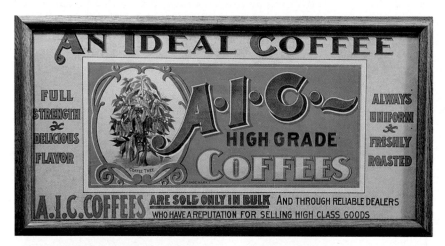

*Buckeye Harvesting Machinery manufactured by Aultman Miller & Co., Akron, Ohio. $1,750.00 – 2,000.00.* Courtesy of Ron Schieber.

*A close-up of the beautiful graphics on the Buckeye Harvesting Poster.*

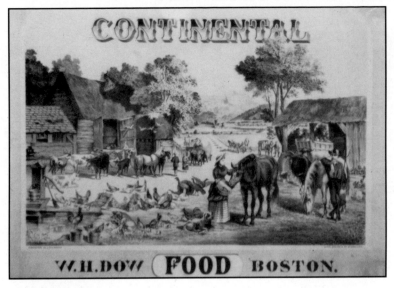

*Store poster for Continental Livestock Food. $375.00 – 450.00.*
Courtesy of Ron Schieber.

*Arm & Hammer Brand Soda, Church & Co. $35.00 – 50.00.*
Wilson Collection.

*Poster advertising Piedmont cigarettes.*
*$275.00 – 450.00.* Courtesy of John & Mary Jo Purdum.

*Large Karo Syrup store*
*sign on canvas. $250.00 –*
*400.00.* Wilson Collection.

*Aristos Flour advertising giveaway. Contains needles. $15.00 – 25.00.* Courtesy of Ron Schieber.

*A beautiful calendar from 1905 with all months displayed. Calendars similar to this one could be imprinted with the name of the general store. $175.00 – 225.00.* Courtesy of Ron Schieber.

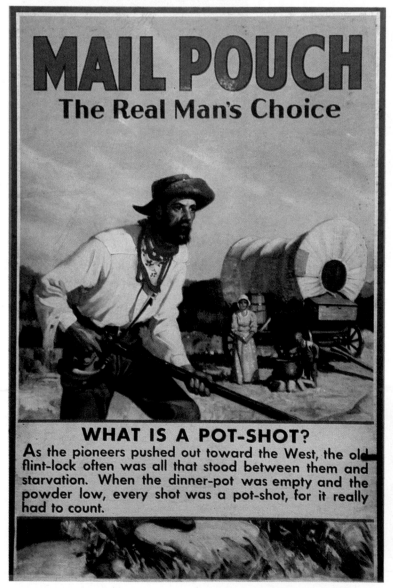

*Mail Pouch — The Real Man's Choice. Typical of the informative posters used by Mail Pouch. This one is particularly interesting because of the Old West theme. $200.00 – 275.00.* Wilson Collection.

*Pinback giveaways depicting Santa Claus and products. $17.00 – 55.00.* Courtesy of Ron Schieber.

*A lady's hatpin package. These were often given to customers who purchased dry goods. $22.00 – 35.00.* Courtesy of Ron Schieber.

*A sample fair poster that could be printed to suit the customer. Fairs were very popular events in the old days and posters were frequently placed in general stores. $525.00 – 750.00.* Courtesy of Ron Schieber.

105

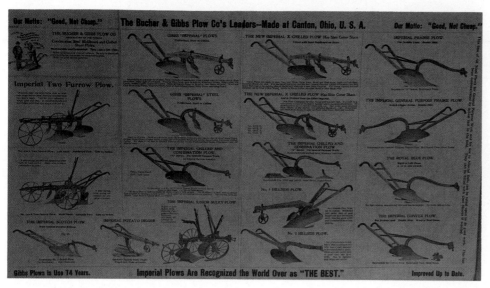

*A large fold-out ad for The Bucher & Gibbs Plow Co. of Canton, Ohio. $8.00 – 15.00.*
Wilson Collection.

*Liberty Blacking giveaway. This one is in remarkable condition and it may have been handed out to celebrate July 4th. It is even equipped with a small bell. $50.00 – 85.00.*
Courtesy of Ron Schieber.

*Golden West Coffee. Large canvas store sign. $135.00 – 250.00.* Wilson Collection.

*David's Prize Soap trade card. The customer was tempted to purchase the soap and find some money when the soap was unwrapped. $4.00 – 8.00.*
Wilson Collection.

*Advertising giveaway for Senora Coffee and Haserot's Fancy Corn. $12.00 – 16.00.* Courtesy of Ron Schieber.

*Star Soap advertising poster. Directions on the poster state that for 25 soap wrappers, the customer can have the picture without advertising. $375.00 – 525.00.* Courtesy of Ron Schieber.

*Clark's Mile-End Spool Cotton poster. $275.00 – 400.00.* Courtesy of Ron Schieber.

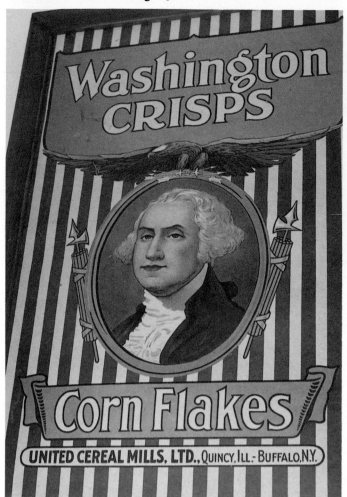

*A small poster advertising the Baltimore Life Insurance Company. General store proprietors sometimes served as agents for insurance companies. $18.00 – 27.00.* Wilson Collection.

*Store sign for Washington Crisps Corn Flakes, United Cereal Mills, Ltd., Quincy, Ill.–Buffalo, New York. $250.00 – 350.00.* Wilson Collection.

*Advertising poster for The Putnam Shoe Company of Berlin, Wisconsin. $125.00 – 175.00.*
Courtesy of Ron Schieber.

*12-month calendar for Fleischmann's Yeast. Dated 1908. $145.00 – 250.00.* Courtesy of Ron Schieber.

*Bear Brand Hosiery postal card. $3.00 – 6.50.* Wilson Collection.

*Laurel Steel Ranges advertising poster. The Art Stove Company. $350.00 – 525.00.* Courtesy of Ron Schieber.

*Advertising trade card for Perry Davis' Pain Killer. $3.00 – 6.00.* Wilson Collection.

*Die-cut 12-month calendar of a beautiful child in a swing. $175.00 – 275.00.* Courtesy of Ron Schieber.

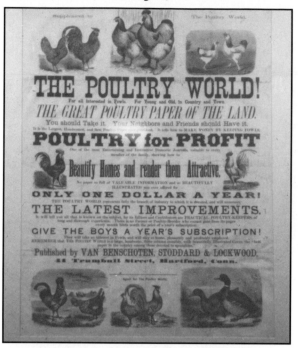

Wood-cut broadside advertising a publication called The Poultry World. *$250.00 – 325.00.* Courtesy of Ron Schieber.

A giveaway for Maccoboy Snuff. The item is a small needle case. *$17.00 – 28.00.* Courtesy of Ron Schieber.

An "American History" calendar with the 12 months of the year printed directly on the calendar. The beautiful women depicted go from American Indian to the Gibson look. *$135.00 – 225.00.* Courtesy of Ron Schieber.

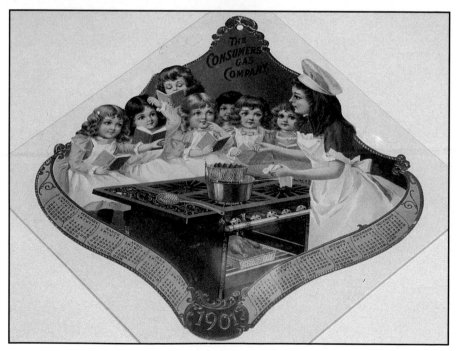

Consumers Gas Company calendar with all 12 months printed directly on the calendar. Dated 1901. *$75.00 – 125.00.* Courtesy of Ron Schieber.

*Pinbacks advertising tobacco products, Cracker Jacks, and other things. $28.00 – 70.00 each.* Courtesy of Ron Schieber.

*1896 calendar for Metropolitan Life. $125.00 – 150.00.* Courtesy of Ron Schieber.

*Various store giveaways including a large Arm & Hammer pencil, Seal Brand Coffee pin case, Rumford pencil, magnifying glass, corkscrew, puzzle, eyeglasses and a McLoughlin school box with the ability to do math functions. $12.00 – 75.00.* Courtesy of Ron Schieber.

*Uncle Sam counter stand-up advertising Wheatlet Breakfast Food. $42.00 – 65.00.* Wilson Collection.

*Horlick's Malted Milk celluloid pocket mirror, $50.00 – 75.00; and another one with a pretty lady, $25.00 – 40.00.* Wilson Collection.

*Stover Manufacturing Co. Bicycle ad. $25.00 – 45.00.* Wilson Collection.

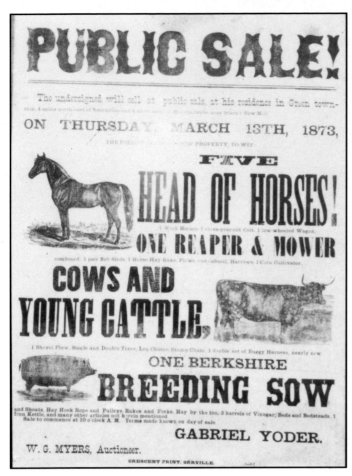

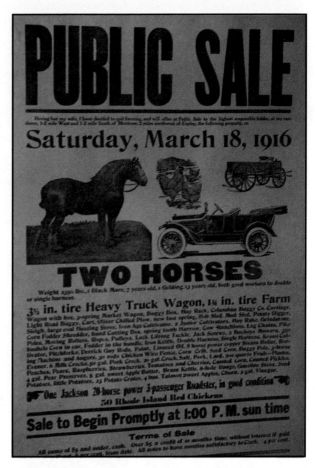

*Auction poster dated March 13, 1873. $135.00 – 215.00.* Courtesy of Ron Schieber.

*Auction Poster dated March 18, 1916. Time had moved on and auction posters were including woodcuts of automobiles along with the horses. $55.00 – 95.00.* Wilson Collection.

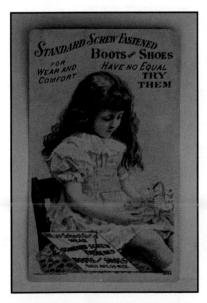

*Advertising trade card for Standard Screw Fastened Boots & Shoes. $2.00 – 5.00.* Wilson Collection.

*Celluloid pocket mirror advertising Bell's Mocha & Java Coffee. J. H. Bell & Co., Chicago. $25.00 – 40.00.* Wilson Collection.

*A celluloid calendar card from The American Art Works, Coshocton, Ohio. 1912. $26.00 – 38.00.* Wilson Collection.

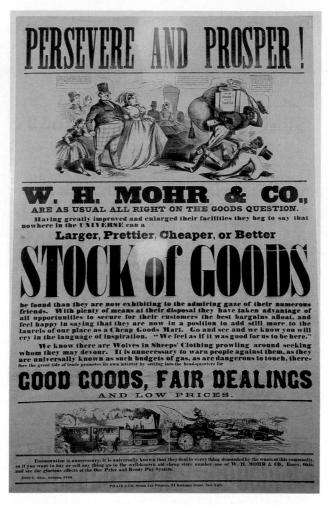

*W. H. Moore & Co. poster advertising their stock of goods. Very early poster. $325.00 – 450.00.* Courtesy of Ron Schieber.

*Metropolitan Insurance Calendar dated 1903. $125.00 – 175.00.* Courtesy of Ron Schieber.

*Lithographed calendar from 1908. Part of a set of 3. $32.00 – 55.00.* Courtesy of Ron Schieber.

*A lithographed paperweight from The Ohio Blue Tip Matches Co., Wadsworth, Ohio. $85.00 – 110.00.* Courtesy of Ron Schieber.

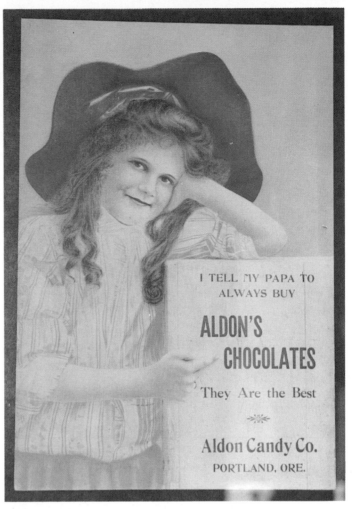

*Aldon's Chocolates advertising poster. Aldon Candy Co., Portland, Oregon. $140.00 – 225.00.* Wilson Collection.

*Pinbacks advertising a variety of products. $35.00 – 75.00.* Courtesy of Ron Schieber.

# Chapter Six
## ❖ THE TOBACCO COUNTER ❖

In the days of the old general store, the tobacco counter was frequently visited and sales were brisk. Every locality had its favorite brands. Containers and boxes were illustrated with beautiful women, historical figures, patriotic and military themes, and domestic animals, to name a few. There were thousands of brands with names like Dixie Kid, Old Abe, Green Turtle, Jack Frost, Prairie Flower, Thunder Clouds, and Wild Fruit.

Of all the tin containers sought, tobacco tins are right at the top. Collectors have had a strong interest in tobacco-related items for years. Cigar store Indians, tobacco tins, advertising posters, cigar boxes and labels, and tobacco novelties are enthusiastically collected.

Cigar smoking in America greatly increased after the Civil War. In the 1880's, cigar smoking became the most popular form of tobacco consumption. It was reported that by the turn of the century, four men in five smoked cigars. From 1880 to 1920, the number of brands available to the public was nothing short of astronomical. As with all methods of early advertising, cigar packaging was very creative and the designs for the box and labels were remarkable. Artistic ingenuity coupled with the lithographic processes of the day brought about embossed, multi-color, and gilded designs. Countless designs were made and the collecting field is wide open for early cigar boxes. It is even possible to find a "one of a kind" box at a relatively modest price.

Plug tobacco was another product that was very popular in the general store. Busy farmers, miners, homesteaders, and cattlemen found chewing tobacco to be very convenient. A store clerk could slice a one pound plug into five or six "cuts" which sold for about 10¢. Flavorings were very popular and licorice, rum, maple sugar, and nutmeg were used to spice up the product.

Once again, store proprietors were encouraged to stock specific brands through use of incentives. Tobacco drummers would offer cigar cutters, counter displays, showcases, lighters and an overabundance of printed matter and premiums. Customers were also heavily targeted and offered everything from giveaways to valuable pre-

*Telonette Cigars advertising sign. Allen Tobacco Co., New York. $425.00 – 750.00.* Courtesy of Ron Schieber.

116

miums. I have an American Tobacco Company Certificate in my collection which declares that "On and after Nov. 15th, 1891, forty of these certificates will entitle you to a Mantel Clock." The description goes on to say that the clock is an eight day clock with cathedral gong and is a perfect time keeper with a value from $12.00 to $15.00. A very tempting offer indeed and one that would certainly help continued sales of the product. The rear of the certificate lists the tobacco products that are accompanied with a certificate.

Virtually every man who walked through the door of the old general store was a potential customer for some form of tobacco product, so the stock of goods was kept plentiful. To keep up with tremendous demand, the companies were producing amazing quantities of tobacco. Lorillard was producing 25 million pounds by

1906. Lorillard's roots reach a long way back in American history. They started business in Manhattan in 1760.

Brand names proliferated in amazing numbers for which today's collector can be thankful. Mountain Dew, Old Hat, Buzz Saw, Poor Man's Comfort, Shoo Fly, Solid Shot, Cheap John, Black Bass, Old Glory, Prune Nugget, and Every Day were just a few of the thousands available.

Because there were so many brands manufactured between 1870 and 1930, tobacco tin container collectors are still finding rare examples of this tribute to the lithographer's art. In addition, the tobacco industry produced huge quantities of advertising signs and posters, cigar cutters and lighters, counter-top displays, showcases, baseball cards, and related items, making this a huge collecting area.

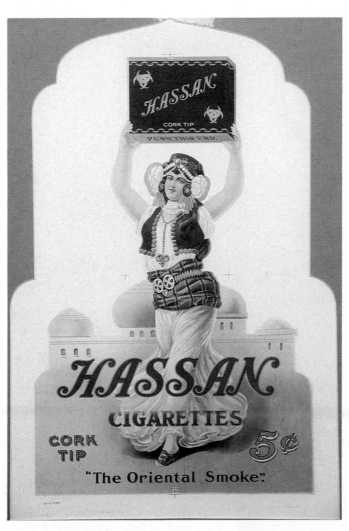

*Hassan Cigarettes die-cut advertising sign. $375.00 – 525.00.* Courtesy of Ron Schieber.

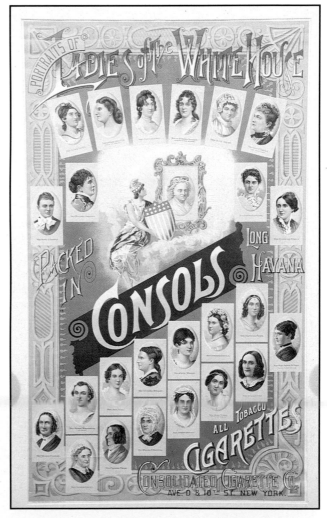

*Consols All Tobacco Cigarettes advertising poster. Portraits of ladies of the White House. Consolidated Cigarette Co., New York. $1,200.00 – 1,500.00.* Courtesy of Ron Schieber.

*Light Sweet Burley; Tiger Chewing Tobacco; Dark Sweet Burley. Round tin containers that were often displayed on the counter. $175.00 – 265.00.* Wilson Collection.

*Game Tobacco store container. Bagley & Co., Detroit, Michigan. $350.00 – 625.00.* Courtesy of John & Mary Jo Purdum.

*Honest Labor Cut Plug tin. R. A. Patterson Co., Richmond, Virginia. $18.00 – 32.00.* Wilson Collection.

*Fastidio High Grade Havana Cigars, Tampa, Florida. $250.00 – 375.00.* Courtesy of Ron Schieber.

*Light & Dark Sweet Cuba round tobacco tins. Spaulding & Merrick, Chicago, $125.00 – 175.00. Sweet Mist Chewing Tobacco, Scotten Dillon Company, Detroit. $125.00 – 225.00.* Courtesy of the El Dorado County Historical Society, Placerville, California.

*Oak-framed Canada Navy advertising poster. It clearly illustrates the need to stock up on Canada Navy products so a late-night visit to the store won't be necessary. $725.00 – 900.00.* Wilson Collection.

*A tobacco-shelf display that includes several of the old-time favorite brands. Union Leader, $22.00 – 45.00; Pedro, $65.00 – 135.00; Dixie Queen, $65.00 – 135.00; Central Union, $45.00 – 75.00; Class, $18.00 – 27.00; Sunset Trail, $165.00 – 375.00; Navy, $65.00 – 95.00; Niggerhair, $100.00 – 225.00; George Washington, $25.00 – 50.00; and Sensation tobacco tins, $22.00 – 45.00.* Courtesy of the El Dorado County Historical Society, Placerville, California.

*A closer look at the tobacco tin display.* Courtesy of the El Dorado County Historical Society, Placerville, California.

An Indian Chief stands vigil at the cigar counter. The cigar store Indian is of recent vintage but very collectible. $275.00 – 500.00. Wilson Collection.

Miners and Puddlers Long Cut Smoking Tobacco. B. Leidersdorf Co., Milwaukee, American Tobacco Company, Successor. Tin pail. $95.00 – 175.00. Wilson Collection.

Tiger Chewing Tobacco. P. Lorillard, New Jersey. $175.00 – 265.00. Sweet Mist Chewing Tobacco cardboard container. Scotten Dillon Company, Detroit. $135.00 – 220.00. Courtesy of the El Dorado County Historical Society, Placerville, California.

*Mayo's Cut Plug tobacco lunch box container. P. H. Mayo & Brothers, Richmond, Virginia. $40.00 – 65.00.* Wilson Collection.

*Chewing tobacco cards. $4.00 – 8.00 each.* Wilson Collection.

*Sure Shot Chewing Tobacco counter-display tin container. Spaulding & Merrick, Chicago. $450.00 – 775.00.* Collection of John and Mary Jo Purdum.

*Germania Star of Cuba and Little Annie Rooney Cigars. Paper ad. Herman & Hedderich, Evansville, Indiana. $575.00 – 850.00.* Wilson Collection.

*Mail Pouch Chewing Tobacco poster. $95.00 – 145.00.* Courtesy of Ron Schieber.

*Advertising sign for Gold Coin Tobacco. $22.00 – 35.00.* Wilson Collection.

*A brick wall of an old store building in the historic gold mining town of Jacksonville, Oregon. Mail Pouch was a very popular brand.*

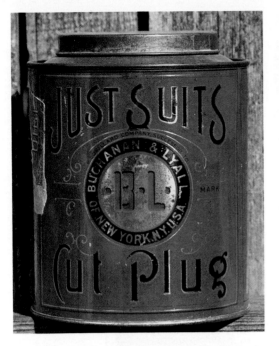

*Just Suits Cut Plug round container. Buchanan & Lyall, New York, P. Lorillard Co., Successor. $75.00 – 125.00.* Wilson Collection.

*Just Suits Cut Plug lunch box tobacco tin. Buchanan & Lyall, New York, P. Lorillard Co., Successor. $55.00 – 85.00.* Wilson Collection.

*Lucky Strike Tobacco tin. R. A. Patterson Tobacco Co., Richmond. $15.00 – 20.00.* Wilson Collection.

*Bagley's Yoc-O-May Hash Cut tobacco tin. Jno. J. Bagley & Co., Detroit. $45.00 – 65.00.* Wilson Collection.

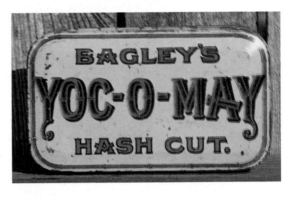

*Silks featuring actresses of the day. Packed in Old Mill Cigarettes. $4.00 – 8.00 each.* Wilson Collection.

*Certificate for a mantel clock from the American Tobacco Company. Circa 1890. $28.00 – 42.00.* Wilson Collection.

*Buckingham Bright Cut Plug Smoking Tobacco tin, John J. Bagley, American Tobacco Co., $25.00 – 75.00; Qboid Granulated Plug tobacco tin, Larus & Bro. Co., Richmond, Virginia, $27.00 – 55.00; Court Royal tobacco tin, San Telmo Cigar Mfg. Co., Detroit, $45.00 – 85.00; Half and Half collapsible tin, The American Tobacco Co., $15.00 – 25.00.* Wilson Collection.

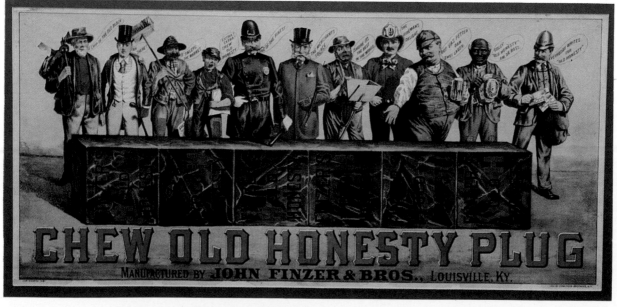

*Chew Old Honesty Plug advertising poster. A very attractive poster with a number of occupations represented. $775.00 – 1,250.00.* Courtesy of Ron Schieber.

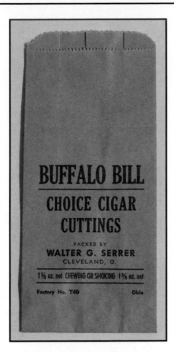

*Bright Tiger Chewing Tobacco tin. P. Lorillard, New Jersey. $50.00 – 75.00.* Wilson Collection.

*Small sack for Buffalo Bill Choice Cigar Cuttings, Walter G. Serrer, Cleveland, Ohio. $1.00 – 3.00.* Wilson Collection.

*Cinco tin container with paper label. Humidor. Otto Eiseniohr & Brothers, Philadelphia. $18.00 – 35.00.* Wilson Collection.

*Kinney Bros. Sweet Caporal Cigarettes advertising poster. New York Standard Cigarettes. $1,000.00 – 1,250.00.* Courtesy of Ron Schieber.

*Kipp's Hand Made Cigars. The Kipp Cigar Co., Hastings, Nebraska.*
*$35.00 – 65.00.* Wilson Collection.

*Fountain Fine Cut Tobacco cake tin.*
*Lovell-Buffington, Covington, Kentucky.*
*$150.00 – 250.00.* Courtesy of John and Mary Jo
Purdum.

*Princess Royal Granulated Mixture tobacco tin. The American Tobacco*
*Company, successor to Wm. S. Kimball & Co. $25.00 – 38.00.* Wilson Collection.

*Orcico Cigars tin. Orrison Cigar Co., Bethesda, Ohio. $275.00 – 575.00.* Wilson Collection.

*Stag Tobacco tin. P. Lorillard, Jersey City, New Jersey. $70.00 – 125.00.* Wilson Collection.

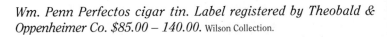

*Wm. Penn Perfectos cigar tin. Label registered by Theobald & Oppenheimer Co. $85.00 – 140.00.* Wilson Collection.

*Tiger lunch box. P. Lorillard Co., Jersey City, New Jersey. $35.00 – 65.00.* Courtesy of Bob Brunswick.

*A fine display of tobacco tins.* Courtesy of John and Mary Jo Purdum.

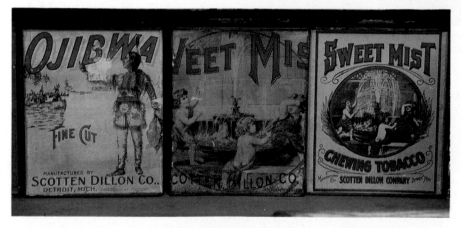

*Ojibwa Fine Cut paper container, $200.00 – 325.00. Sweet Mist, Sweet Mist Chewing Tobacco, paper containers, $125.00 – 225.00. All manufactured by Scotten Dillon Co., Detroit.* Courtesy of John and Mary Jo Purdum.

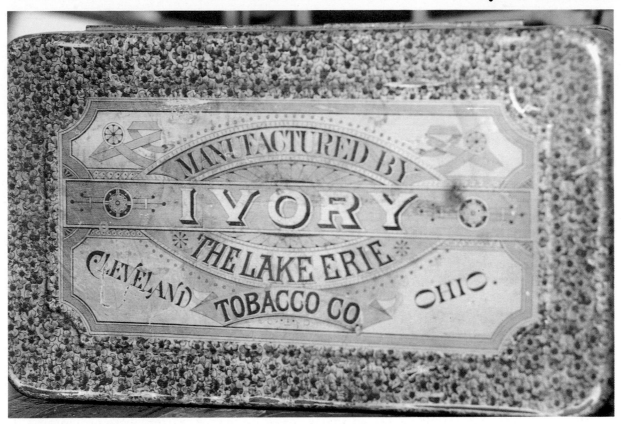

*Ivory tobacco tin. Manufactured by The Lake Erie Tobacco Company, Cleveland, Ohio. $80.00 – 115.00.* Wilson Collection.

*Option tobacco tin. Factory No 436, 18th Dist., Ohio. The cigars are 3 for 5¢ and declared to be mild and pleasant. $65.00 – 95.00.* Wilson Collection.

*Genuine Sweet Cuba Fine Cut chewing tobacco. Counter display. Spaulding & Merrick, Chicago. $300.00 – 500.00.* Courtesy of Bob Brunswick.

# Chapter Seven
## ⊹ CHRISTMAS AT THE GENERAL STORE ⊹

No holiday in America is more antici-pated than Christmas. The heritage has been with us for years and was thriving in the days of the old general store. It was a time for the entire family to visit the crossroads store and marvel at the new stock of holiday goods. The Christmas season was pure enchantment for children and the local merchant enjoyed stocking up on merchandise of special interest to boys and girls.

The store took on a magical quality. Barrels and bins were moved from their accustomed places along with other familiar merchandise to make way for a special display of toys and other tempting treasures. A table might be placed in the aisle to call attention to eager young eyes. The customary loungers around the old stove might discover some of their space had been

appropriated. Dolls, buggies, story books, games, and candy were prominently displayed. Other items would often be placed in showcases with regular merchandise.

The local newspaper considered the arrival of holiday goods to be worthy of reporting. Once the news was out, it was time for the country family to load up the youngsters along with whatever the family had for trade and make a trip to the store.

When economic times were tough, presents were something useful or edible. As times improved, children looked forward to the many tempting toys and games that a number of growing manufacturers were providing.

Of particular delight were the colorful games with brightly lithographed covers and filled with fun and imagination. Since the beginning days of my collecting, I've always been intrigued and delighted with board games. The colorful box covers rival quality advertising prints and posters plus provide the bonus of some very fascinating games. This area of col-lecting has been overlooked until recently. Two reported sales emphasize that point. The "Man on the Moon" game (1901) was auctioned off at $4,600.00 and a McLoughlin Brothers "Bulls and Bears — The Great Wall St. Game" recently sold for $28,000.00! The good news is that there are a number of great examples of early games still available to collectors at reasonable prices. These wonderful collectibles are now consid-ered little boxes of history.

The period from the 1880's through 1920 has become recognized as the Golden Age of Board Games. That period closely parallels the glory days of the old general store. The big

*Santa Claus Game. This is an unusual Santa cover not only due to Santa's yellow tights; it is one of the very few Santa game cov-ers that features actual (produced) games. Most other Santa games show primarily toys. 9" x 15", c. 1905, Parker Brothers. $500.00 – 900.00.* Courtesy of Patrice McFarland.

three, McLoughlin Brothers, Parker Brothers, and Milton Bradley, competed wildly during those years to capture and keep shares of the market. Games were bigger, brighter, and more elaborate, containing beautifully illustrated boards, splendid pieces, and topped by even more gloriously illustrated covers. Advances in the use of chromolithography escalated the competition.

That the popularity and beauty of the old board games peaked during the golden era of the country store is no coincidence. Reconstruction, westward expansion, the gilded age of great fortunes and prosperity had effects throughout the nation. Progress and extreme poverty co-existed. New towns and businesses boomed and fell like fireworks. The country was becoming connected by railroad lines and wagon roads went just about anywhere. Goods were transported across the continent. A board game or other toy could stand a fair chance of brightening a child's Christmas in Jacksonville, Oregon; Cripple Creek, Colorado; or Peachum, Vermont.

The games chronicled every aspect of changing America from trains and business to the growing popularity of baseball. Everything and anything was possible and anything imaginable appeared on these boxes.

Of all the special Christmas toys that appeared at the store, nothing offered more fun and imagination than the board games. It is a tribute to the love and respect that children had for the games that so many have survived in outstanding condition. Those little hands lovingly cared for their games and many are now being enjoyed by today's collector. Game collecting has emerged as a fast-growing area of the antique toy market.

We have fond memories of looking at toys when we were children. I have to feel, however, it must have been a very special time in the period from 1870 to 1930 to view the toys on display at the old general store. Bright-faced and fancy dressed bisque dolls, cast iron mechanical banks and tin toys with that great smell of new paint, colorful books, and puzzles just waiting for discovery. But the old board games had something unique to offer. They could be shared with friends and be the source of adventure, imagination, challenge, and just plain fun!

Kindred spirits to the old board games were the early children's books. The books were produced by a number of companies including McLoughlin Brothers, Graham & Matlack, Dana Estes & Co., and the M. A. Donohue & Co. The covers had a variety of themes from fables to

*The Exciting, Laughable, New Game Pillow-Dex. An early balloon-toss type of game, Pillow-Dex comes with a string to stretch midway across a dining room table, anchor blocks and a rather curious "Bladder" or balloon. Entertainment for evenings in the home parlor, Pillow-Dex no doubt liberated even the most tightly wound spirits. 7" x 5¼", 1896, Parker Brothers. $35.00 – 85.00.* Courtesy of Patrice McFarland.

*Bowling/A Board Game. This astonishing cover illustration graphically depicts women's love of the sport despite the oddity of playing in restrictive dress. This game is one of the very few bowling games made that illustrates women at their leisure. 15½" x 12", 1896, Parker Brothers. $75.00 – 175.00.* Courtesy of Patrice McFarland.

from fables to Santa Claus. The covers were beautifully illustrated with many charming scenes of children engaged in various activities. I have a number of children's books in my collection and I'm always fascinated by discovering little sketches, drawings, and writings placed in the books by some child of yesteryear. These books remain plentiful and can be acquired by the collector at relatively modest amounts. I expect that values will continue to rise. I have a book from 1914 with the original price of 25¢ inside the cover. I note that I paid $9.00 for it a few years back and it is presently worth about $18.00. Many of the children's books have wonderful color plates inside the book. One that comes to mind is a McLoughlin *The Night Before Christmas or a Visit of St. Nicholas.* The book is mounted on linen and contains some wonderfully colored lithographs on the inside pages. It is a real prize.

The old general store carried an incredible variety of candy. Jars, buckets, containers, and display cases offered the old favorites as well as the newest sensation in confections. Stick candy, rock candy, lemon drops, Arabian gum drops, Gibraltars, licorice, and several flavors of tasty lozenges were just a few of the treats available. Collectors have numerous confection-related containers to seek out. Glass candy display jars of every imaginable size, candy and gum boxes, tin containers, and small oak and glass display cases now tempt the collector instead of the early store customer who sought to satisfy a sweet tooth.

Just about every little girl yearned for a doll and the country merchant was certain to include several in his Christmas stock to attract eager young eyes. Dolls with heads of bisque (unglazed porcelain) and composition bodies were in demand. Others were fabricated from glazed porcelain, wood, poured wax, cloth, and papier-mâché. To move up from a beloved hand-made muslin rag doll to an honest-to-goodness store bought doll from Santa Claus was something special. The importation of German bisque dolls was prolific and there was an astounding variety on the market at the turn of the century. As an example, the Sears, Roebuck and Co. catalog for Fall 1900 offers a stylishly dressed doll with bisque head and flowing hair,

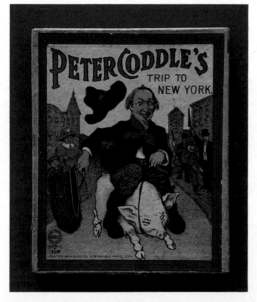

*Peter Coddle's Trip to New York. One of the most common games. Peter Coddle appeared for decades in a seemingly endless variety, most often dressed as a country bumpkin but later assuming grander roles. Peter Coddle made his way almost everywhere. Each game had a book or story about the particular adventure with humorous slips to be drawn and read whenever a blank line appeared in the tale, as it was read aloud. 5½" x ¾", c. 1900, Milton Bradley. $35.00 – 75.00.* Courtesy of Patrice McFarland.

*The Great Game of Pharaoh's Frogs. It's what's inside the box that makes this game so extraordinary. Inside are twelve very stylized, almost sculptural, stamped and painted metal frogs with bent brass wire legs. Very unusual. This is one of the few games produced by Ives, Blakeslee & Williams who were known as one of the greatest producers of quality toys in America at the time. 6¼" x 6¼", 1891, Ives, Blakeslee & Williams. $200.00 – 400.00.* Courtesy of Patrice McFarland.

steady eyes, jointed body, pretty costume, and a length of 12 inches for 25¢. Similar dolls were available at the friendly general store.

As competition increased from specialty toy stores and the catalogs, and the automobile began to replace horse transportation, the toy salesman's stops at the old general store became less frequent. The familiar display of Christmas toys at the crossroads store was beginning to disappear. There finally came a time when the traditional toy display was all but non-existent.

The thrill of a visit to see the store's holiday goods brightened the Christmas season of countless children years ago. The memories linger on. The old mercantile store has passed into the parade of history, but the heritage remains for collectors to enjoy.

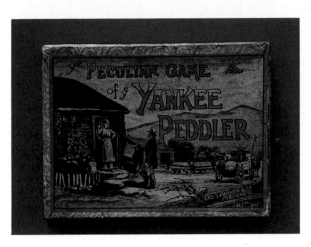

*Ye Peculiar Game of Ye Yankee Peddler. An early game of the trades; large cards with nice illustrations of priced goods and small type only cards with prices of foodstuffs and home products. 6½" x 5", c. 1890, George S. Parker. $70.00 – 125.00.* Courtesy of Patrice McFarland.

*The Black Cat Fortune Telling Game. Great illustrations on not just the box but the cards as well makes this a striking favorite in any collection and especially if the collector loves cats. 6¾" x 5", 1897, Parker Brothers. $100.00 – 200.00.* Courtesy of Patrice McFarland.

*Toy Town School. A truly wonderful playset complete with everything needed to conduct a country school. Included are a (cardboard) blackboard, wooden drawing board, T-square and triangles, metal pencil sharpener; school bell, teacher's spectacles and lots of printed class lessons, report cards and the like. All in miniature for little hands, of course! 18¼" x 14½", c. 1911, Milton Bradley. $200.00 – 400.00.* Courtesy of Patrice McFarland.

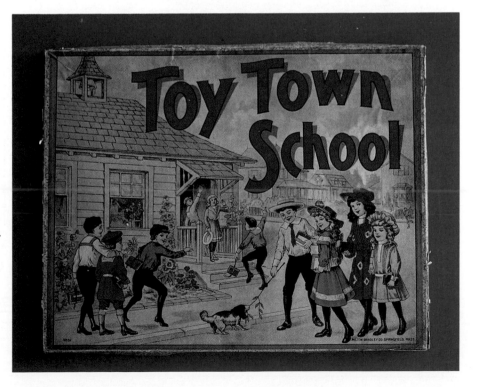

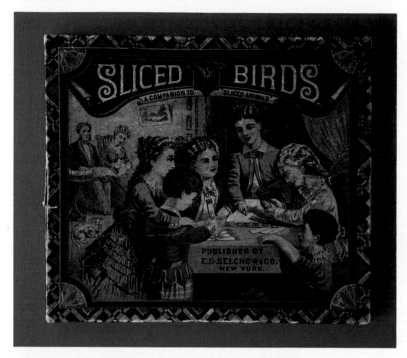

*Sliced Birds. Both a game and a puzzle. Selchow put out many different themes based on this format. Printed on cardboard and sliced into strips, these pictures when reassembled would show both the word and the image of various birds, animals, plants, flowers, machines, etc. 9¼" x 8", c. 1875, E. G. Selchow & Co. $50.00 – 150.00.* Courtesy of Patrice McFarland.

*A fancy candy box. $30.00 – 48.00.* Wilson Collection.

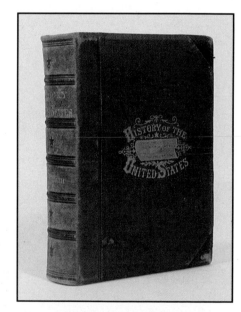

History Of The United States; From the Discovery of America To The Present Time. *Published in 1876. A Christmas gift for the serious student of history. $20.00 – 35.00.* Wilson Collection.

The Night Before Christmas. *Linen child's book, c. 1900, Graham & Matlock, New York. $45.00 – 85.00.* Courtesy of Twinsburg Historical Society.

*Grandmama's Improved Game of Useful Knowledge. "Grandmama's" games were put out in many variations by most companies and were evolutions of earlier bible study games. The character of Grandmama provided the generational link and matriarchal approval of playing games. The games were usually the question and answer type with a small book and question cards. 6¼" x 4⅜", c. 1895, McLoughlin Brothers. $35.00 – 85.00.* Courtesy of Patrice McFarland.

*New Game of Migration. This excellent cover illustration begins to show some consciousness about Native Americans (of course, in 1890 they are* not *willingly migrating). The board inside is not themed with the cover but is a strategy game with colorful society caricatures in the corners. It is very common to have seemingly mismatched game boxes and contents. Games that have a strong theme throughout often have a higher value. 8¾" x 16½", 1890, McLoughlin Brothers. $375.00 – 750.00.* Courtesy of Patrice McFarland.

*Child's doll buggy. This one retains its original color and decals, c. 1890. $500.00 – 750.00.* Courtesy of the Twinsburg Historical Society.

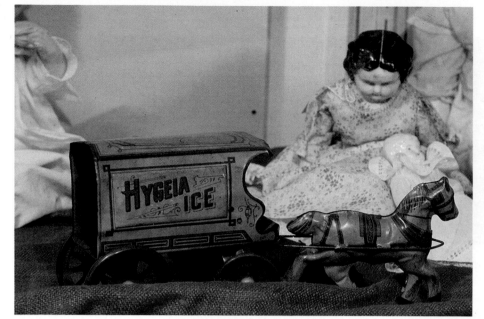

*Tin toy. Hygeia Ice Wagon and Horse, $225.00 – 275.00. China doll, $250.00 – 500.00.* Courtesy of the Twinsburg Historical Society.

*Three bisque dolls. $275.00 – 600.00 each.* Courtesy of the Twinsburg Historical Society.

*Bank of Good Fortune. A Christmas giveaway that was handed out in a general store to faithful customers. 1908. $12.00 – 22.00.* Wilson Collection.

*Sunny Monday Washing Set. Sunny Monday was a real brand of soap sold long ago in most country stores. The outstanding condition of this set suggests that some bright young girl knew just what realistic lessons lay beneath the box cover and opened it infrequently. 8½" x 13½", c. 1910, Parker Brothers. $150.00 – 325.00.*
Courtesy of Patrice McFarland.

*Bradley's Toy Village. The largest of the toy village sets, this box contains some 14 "put together" cardboard buildings, a mat to play on which is printed with roads and a pond, cut-out boats, fences, trees, wagons, and people all ready to be placed in small metal stands, creating a splendid town scene. Buildings include many fine homes, a cabin, a hotel, a school, churches, and a blacksmith shop ready to welcome any child's imagination. Some buildings sport illustrations of children playing blocks, hoops, jump rope, and other outdoor games of the day. 14½" x 19½", c. 1905, Milton Bradley. $200.00 – 400.00.* Courtesy of Patrice McFarland.

*New and Improved Fish Pond Game. This classic fishpond game has 4 wooden poles with brass hooks, numerous fish that are numbered for scoring points and a box with a raised platform "pond," slotted to hold fish for catching. It's harder than you think! 17¾" x 8", 1890, McLoughlin Brothers. $125.00 – 200.00.* Courtesy of Patrice McFarland.

*A beautiful die-cut Santa Claus with children and toys that was given out by Drewes Bros. Fairmount Market. $125.00 – 175.00.* Wilson Collection.

*Right Above:* Rhymes and Chimes From Mother Goose. *Child's book. M. A. Donohue & Co., Chicago. $22.00 – 35.00.* Wilson Collection.

*Right Below:* Girls' and Boys' Budget of Stories. *Child's book. McLoughlin Brothers, New York. $24.00 – 38.00.* Wilson Collection.

*Puzzle depicting an early fire engine on the way to a fire. $55.00 – 85.00.* Wilson Collection.

138

Puss in Boots and Other Stories. *Child's book. McLoughlin Brothers, 1902. $22.00 – 34.00.* Wilson Collection.

*Illustration on the rear cover of the McLoughlin Puss in Boots book.*

Jolly Times Painting Book. *Graham & Matlack, New York. 1912. $22.00 – 32.00.* Wilson Collection.

*Inside the cover of the Jolly Times book. The child had the illustration on the left to use as a guide to paint the one on the right.*

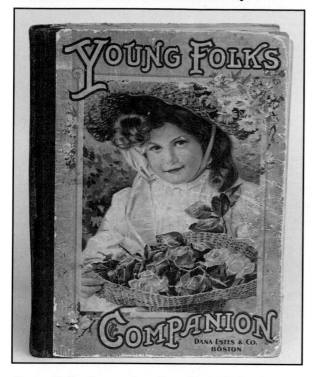

Home Painting Book. *McLoughlin Brothers, New York. $22.00 – 28.00.* Wilson Collection.

Young Folks Companion. *Dana Estes & Co., Boston. Child's book. $20.00 – 26.00.* Wilson Collection.

Fun With Paint And Brush. *Graham & Matlack, New York. $22.00 – 28.00.* Wilson Collection.

*Inside the book showing illustrations of early toys. The little owner of this book never got around to doing any painting on this page.* Wilson Collection.

*For the young readers looking for adventures in the Old West,* Daring Donald McKay or The Last War Trail of the Modocs *was available for 25¢. $20.00 – 32.00.* Wilson Collection.

*Game Of Success. A variation of the Horatio Alger theme by a lesser known company. Although not as elaborate a game as other examples, the cover treatment is quite striking. It has a built-in platform board. 9½" x 10½", c. 1910, J. Ottman Lith. $65.00 – 120.00.* Courtesy of Patrice McFarland.

*The Trolley Came Off/A Comical Game. This card game is one of the smaller Parker Brothers trolley games. Trolley games are quite rare and are therefore of higher value than some more common games of their time. 6½" x 5", c. 1900, Parker Brothers. $70.00 – 165.00.* Courtesy of Patrice McFarland.

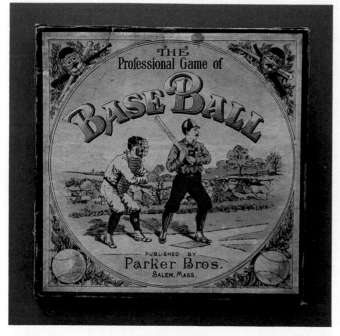

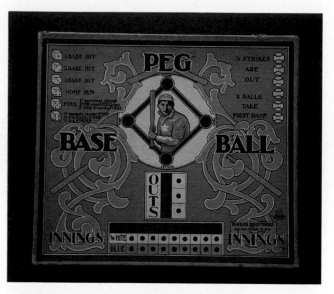

The Professional Game of Base Ball. Box bottom board of a baseball diamond and wonderful cover art of early players make this a great piece. The illustrations represent nicely the uniforms and equipment used at the time. 8¼" square, 1889, Parker Brothers. $275.00 – 525.00. Courtesy of Patrice McFarland.

Peg Baseball. Although this game does not have specific player or team tie-ins, it is a fine example of the popular baseball games of its time and is bright and colorful. It was published for many years. 12" x 10¾", c. 1920, Parker Brothers. $125.00 – 225.00. Courtesy of Patrice McFarland.

A Trip To Washington. Along the lines of Peter Coddle, this game came with a booklet to be read aloud that sporadically offered blank spaces and a stack of slips with short sayings or words that were drawn and read aloud to fill in the blanks. 3¾" x 4¾", c. 1880, Milton Bradley. $28.00 – 58.00.

Courtesy of Patrice McFarland.

Post Card Game. A very specific theme and hard-to-find quality illustration of a woman on the job makes this game highly cross-collectible by postcard enthusiasts and historians alike. 5¼" x 7¼", c. 1905, J. Ottman Lith. $62.00 – 110.00. Courtesy of Patrice McFarland.

Commerce. The great cover art is what no doubt sold this simple match-up card game based on trading commodities. 4⅝" x 6¼", c. 1900, J. Ottman Lith. $32.00 – 58.00. Courtesy of Patrice McFarland.

*Dissected Outline Map of the United States of America. Dissected maps and map games are very common but the early ones are interesting historically. Often they contain maps with Indian territories and were produced prior to statehood for many of the states west of the Mississippi. Can be litho on wood or heavy cardboard. They are also sought after by puzzle collectors. 8½" x 6½", c. 1880, Milton Bradley. $32.00 – 80.00.* Courtesy of Patrice McFarland.

*Little Goldenlocks and the Three Bears. Exceptional illustration, box bottom board and themed spinner with bears. Games are often based on well-known children's tales and early books. 10½" x 19¾", 1890, McLoughlin Brothers. $525.00 – 1,050.00.* Courtesy of Patrice McFarland.

*Game of Snap. Snap games are quite common and are basic match-up card games. Covers and cards offer everything from human comical characters to machines to frogs to other themes. 4½" x 5¼", c. 1910, Milton Bradley. $18.00 – 55.00.* Courtesy of Patrice McFarland.

*Corn and Beans/The Funniest Game Out. Believe it or not, this game is actually played with corn kernels and beans as pieces. Long forgotten games, tucked away decades ago in dresser drawers and attic trunks, are often found devoid of their pieces and chewed right through by hungry mice. 5½" x 3½", c. 1875, E. G. Selchow & Co. $24.00 – 56.00.* Courtesy of Patrice McFarland.

*Game of Business or Going to Work. Variation on the Horatio Alger theme. This cover also shows a woman at work. Separate one-piece board lifts out of the box. 14" x 13", 1895, Parker Brothers. $225.00 – 325.00.* Courtesy of Patrice McFarland.

*Fun at the Circus. Wonderful circus cover illustrations make this a valued game. The box-bottom board is a chutes and ladders style of play. Very colorful and sweet representations of animals are realistic in style. The spinner has a smiling dog at its center. 17" x 17", 1897, McLoughlin Brothers. $525.00 – 950.00.* Courtesy of Patrice McFarland.

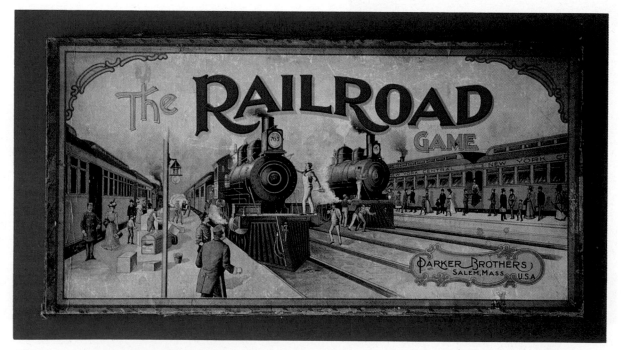

*The Railroad Game. One of the greatest railroad covers; direct view of trains in an arrival/departure setting in wide angle perspective. Box bottom board is track style game. 20¼" x 10½", c. 1896, Parker Brothers. $450.00 – 1,050.00.* Courtesy of Patrice McFarland.

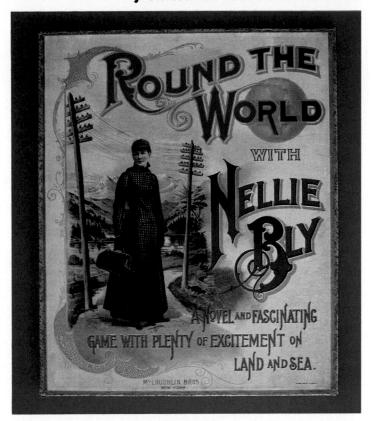

Round the World with Nellie Bly. One of the most undervalued games in McLoughlin's line, especially the large box version. Nellie Bly is of true historical nature. Elizabeth Cochrane (her real name) was a newspaper reporter, businesswoman, entrepreneur and world traveler who beat Jules Verne's travel record around the world among her many other accomplishments. 16" x 19½", 1890, McLoughlin Brothers. $325.00 – 650.00. Courtesy of Patrice McFarland.

*Game of the District Messenger Boy or Merit Rewarded. Many games were based on the Horatio Alger themes. This one has wonderful metal messenger boy pieces and a spinner that mounts onto the gameboard. It is a more common game to find but is very well produced. 9" x 17½", 1905, McLoughlin Brothers. $225.00 – 375.00.* Courtesy of Patrice McFarland.

*The Sociable Telephone/A Game for the Smart Set. A nice cross-collectible theme and quality illustration of a period oak wall phone in use. There are a number of telephone games from the era but this is one of the most interesting. 8½" x 6¾", c. 1902, J. Ottman Lith. $50.00 – 100.00.* Courtesy of Patrice McFarland.

*Fancy candy box. $17.00 – 35.00.* Wilson Collection.

*Fancy candy box. $12.00 – 24.00.* Wilson Collection.

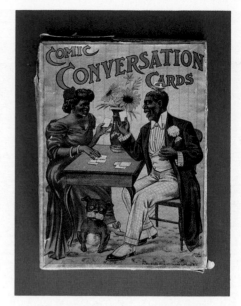

*Comic Conversation Cards. There are two versions, nearly identical, of this game. One has an Anglo-American couple and the other has an African-American couple. Both couples are posed, dressed and presented similarly. 5½" x 7", c. 1900, J. Ottman Lith. $60.00 – 115.00.* Courtesy of Patrice McFarland.

*Athletic Sports. Great track and field cover shows runners in uniform. A smaller game but not a common theme and it has a wonderful spinner dotted with stars. 13" x 8", c. 1905, Parker Brothers. $60.00 – 110.00.* Courtesy of Patrice McFarland.

*The Amusing Game of the Corner Grocery. Wonderful little game of buying and selling from the first decade of Parker games. Small cardboard squares for money and product cards showing nice store scenes and cuts of spices, staples, chocolates, matches, soap, kerosene, blueing, etc. 6½" x 5", 1887, George S. Parker. $55.00 – 95.00.* Courtesy of Patrice McFarland.

*Ocean to Ocean Flight Game. The illustration on this game is both beautiful and ethereal. The scalloped wing and orange coloring lends much to the air of fantasy of this early flight game. Box bottom board shows map of route. 7½" x 12¼", c. 1925, Wilder. $60.00 – 115.00.* Courtesy of Patrice McFarland.

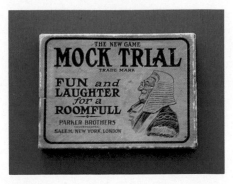

Table Ring Game. This skill and action game has very bright and colorful rings pressed and cut out of cardboard which would be tossed at a turned, painted wooden post "target" with base. 8¾" x 8½", c. 1890, Milton Bradley. $32.00 – 85.00. Courtesy of Patrice McFarland.

Mock Trial. For a riotous evening, friends and family would play this entertaining, theatrical game while acting out the silly and often hilarious testimony. Invented by Elizabeth Magie Phillips who is the inventor and patentee of The Landlord's Game, aka Monopoly, Finance, Easy Money, Fortune, etc. Her 1910 Mock Trial game establishes her very early connections with Parker Brothers. 6½" x 5", 1910, Parker Brothers. $25.00 – 80.00. Courtesy of Patrice McFarland.

Ping Pong. This is a very early version of the now classic game. Parker Brothers proclaimed they had secured the rights and were the sole authorized sellers from the London producers. An early monopolization of a popular game. 20" x 8", c. 1905, Parker Brothers. $125.00 – 215.00. Courtesy of Patrice McFarland.

Post Office Game. Another game/play set from the "Toy Town" lines, this set has all the parts shown as well as numerous additional stamps, coins, sheets, envelopes, postcards and telegrams, all set for the postal office of the past. 9¾" x 14", c. 1910, Parker Brothers. $75.00 – 175.00. Courtesy of Patrice McFarland.

*Cooking School For Little Girls. "Sweet!" is truly the best word to describe this play set. Yes, there is real flour in the sack and real postum in the box. It's surprising that it lasted through the century still intact, but what a wonderful piece to come upon at a local auction! Who knows what young chef played her way to culinary mastery! 8½" x 13", c. 1910, Parker Brothers. $135.00 – 265.00.* Courtesy of Patrice McFarland.

*The Errand Boy or Failure and Success. This is one of the largest box bottom board versions of the Horatio Alger themed games. Excellent cover graphics and lots of lessons and luck. 14½" x 15", 1891, McLoughlin Brothers. $475.00 – 875.00.* Courtesy of Patrice McFarland.

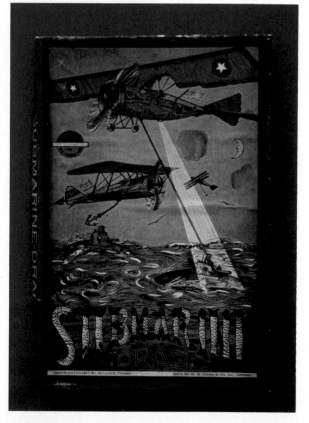

*Submarine Drag. Before we knew the limitations of airplanes or submarines this cover illustration gave us one daunting application. Here are planes, flying low over the ocean, at night no less, fishing submarines out of the water with ships' anchors lowered on ropes and used as hooks. Wow! The game is a fish pond style with cardboard cut-out planes ready to hook cardboard subs out of the cardboard ocean. Fish spell out the title. 7¼" x 10¾", 1919, Willis G. Young. $75.00 – 135.00.* Courtesy of Patrice McFarland.

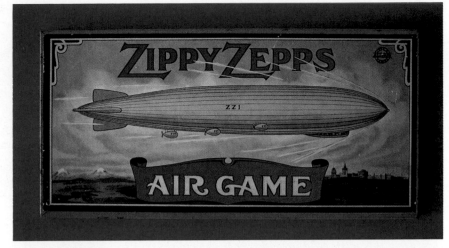

*Zippy Zepps Air Game. Zippy Zepps is far and away the best zeppelin themed game and has an outstanding cover. The pieces are small metal zeppelins and moves are made by drawing numbered cards. The board shows various stopping points from New York to London to Paris to Berlin to Washington and is as bright and colorful as the cover. 18" x 9", c. 1920, All-Fair (Alderman Fairchild). $425.00 – 825.00.* Courtesy of Patrice McFarland.

*Combat. A generic battle strategy game. Box bottom board is grid pattern and moves are made combat/strategy style somewhat like Halma or Chinese Checkers. 15" x 9", c. 1900, Milton Bradley. $60.00 – 115.00.* Courtesy of Patrice McFarland.

*A New Game Skirmish At Harper's Ferry. A fine example of a game made after the Civil War but about a specific battle or event. Superb illustrations on both the box label and board. It is a strategy game with chess like pieces. Black sets up on one side of the board and white on the other to win the battle and take prisoners. 16" x 15", 1891, McLoughlin Brothers. $525.00 – 875.00.* Courtesy of Patrice McFarland.

*Radio Game. The airwaves crackle again when you view this wonderful graphic cover showing an early radio set and electrified radio signal style lettering. The "Lis'nin In" cards display the call letters of radio stations around the country. 7½" x 4¾", c. 1920, Parker Brothers. $27.00 – 58.00.* Courtesy of Patrice McFarland.

*Game of Checkers, Backgammon, and Tousel. McLoughlin had a specific line of "bookcase style" or folding, slipcased games. They were often 2 or 3 games in one and had a pieces box inside and a block spinner. (Spinner not shown.) These were produced primarily in the 1870's – 1890's and then phased out as they were quite expensive to produce. 7½" x 14" x 2", Open Boards: 14" x 14" x 1", 1877, McLoughlin Brothers. $75.00 – 175.00.* Courtesy of Patrice McFarland.

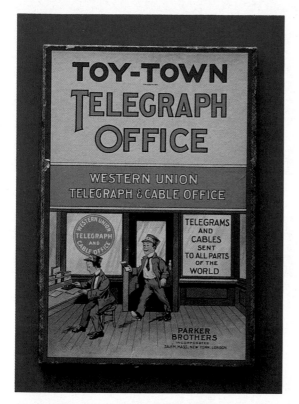

*Toy Town Telegraph. Toy Town play sets were considered games in the broad sense and often covered the same themes as games. This telegraph set contains elaborate pieces such as masks, telegrapher's window, envelopes, stamps, telegrams and appropriate mechanisms like signal senders and telegraph poles. They lent themselves to very imaginative play. 9⅜" x 13⅞", c. 1910, Parker Brothers. $125.00 – 220.00.* Courtesy of Patrice McFarland.

*Checkered Game of Life. Here is an example of Milton Bradley's first game. It takes one back to the earlier morality games of European descent. The goal is to go from Infancy to Happy Old Age without landing on the pitfalls of crime, disgrace, idleness or suicide! 13" x 13⅜" board, parts box 4¾" x 3¾", 1866, Milton Bradley. $55.00 – 185.00.* Courtesy of Patrice McFarland.

*Above: The Amusing Game Heedless Tommy. This game is truly one of McLoughlin Brothers best! Not only is the box gorgeous, as is the board with its great illustrations and golden squares, but the theme is honorable and teaches lessons of the Society for the Prevention of Cruelty to Animals. As the title states, Tommy is indeed a heedless fellow and is cruel to the animals he comes upon. In this game, however, Tommy gets his due and the animals give him a dose of his own medicine! Hopefully he learns his lesson. 9⅜" x 20", 1893, McLoughlin Brothers. $525.00 – 1,050.00. Above Right: The beautiful illustrated board.* Courtesy of Patrice McFarland.

*Game of Round the World. Early in the company's history, Milton Bradley produced some wonderfully illustrated and lithographed games. The large board shown here is one of the absolute best and shows vignettes of sailing ships of all kinds which make a spiraling pattern around New York harbor. 18½" x 18½" (board), 1875, Milton Bradley. $225.00 – 425.00.* Courtesy of Patrice McFarland.

*Little Toy Town Grocery Store. Every budding general store owner must have had this play set! From the real miniature product samples on the shelves to the little proprietress on the box you can almost feel the wooden floor boards under your feet and hear the change hit the counter as you play a game of store. (Notice the Shaker woman on the box.) 8½" x 10½", c. 1910, Parker Brothers. $135.00 – 250.00.* Courtesy of Patrice McFarland.

*Left: Little Shoppers (board; no box shown) box 14¼" x 11½". Wonderful product/brand name game with pie-cut pieces (on stands) of products. Some of the products are still in use today such as Gorton's Codfish, Necco Wafers, Pillsbury Flour, Ivory Soap, Black Cat Heels, Dutch Boy Paints. 1915, Gibson Game Co. $225.00 – 425.00. Right: Little Shoppers board detail, 13½" x 20".* Courtesy of Patrice McFarland.

*Little Shoppers die-cut pieces detail.*

*Trolley Car Game. $165.00 – 280.00.* Courtesy of Patrice McFarland.

*Devoe Water Colors. Tin box. Devoe & Raynolds Co., Inc., founded 1754. $12.00 – 25.00.* Wilson Collection.

*Game of the Visit of Santa Claus. One of the finest early Christmas games ever made. Unlike many early board games that boasted a beautifully illustrated box lid and a much less interesting playing board inside, this early game features equally attractive illustrations on the board of Santa Claus preparing to visit children's homes on Christmas Eve. 10½" x 19½", McLoughlin Brothers. $725.00 – 1,350.00. Below: The wonderful board that goes with the game.* Courtesy of Patrice McFarland.

*An early die-cut stand-up Santa Claus that was used to draw attention to the general store's toy display. $90.00 – 155.00.* Wilson Collection.

*Geschäft or the Game of Business. Another one of the rare and desirable games. Great cover graphics, c. 1895, Chaffree & Selchow. $350.00 – 700.00.* Courtesy of Patrice McFarland.

# Chapter Eight
## ❖ CARE & RESTORATION ❖

I recall visiting an antique shop in the Gold Rush country of California one hot day in July. Displayed in the window were several choice tobacco tins and a fine Honest Scrap advertising sign. In talking with the dealer, I learned that the items had been recently placed on display to attract attention. None of the items were for sale. The heavy July rays of the sun were making direct contact with the collectibles. In a diplomatic way, I suggested to the shop owner that Father Sol was no friend of early advertising pieces and that irreversible damage would occur in time. I returned a few months later and was dismayed to see the items still in the window. All of the tins and the advertising sign had been in remarkable condition. The deterioration that had taken place saddened me. The tobacco tins and the Honest Scrap sign had faded substantially along with their values.

A word to the wise collector. Even in indirect sunlight, damage will occur in time. Try to recall the last time you visited an outstanding museum. You will remember that the sun was not an invited guest. Although our homes and offices are not museums, reasonable precautions should be taken to protect valued tins and advertising art.

*Honest Scrap Tobacco advertising sign on cardboard. Severe damage. Shows evidence of moisture exposure and other damage. Can this interesting sign be saved?* Courtesy of Chuck Kovacic.

## CARE AND CLEANING

Due to differences in paints, the aging process and other factors, there is no universally safe method of cleaning. Extreme care should be used in cleaning tin and wood containers and tin advertising signs. The intelligent rule is: *if in doubt, don't do it.* I have purchased tin containers that appeared to be in poor condition but were simply dirty. A good cleaning and wax application brought the tin to its true bright condition. I suggest that before beginning to wash a tin container, test a small area with a cloth dampened in a mild soap or cleaner without ammonia. Rinse off the solution as you work. This will lessen the possibility of fading. If the item should have a desirable patina, you should reconsider cleaning. Improper cleaning can reduce a desirable and salable item to one of little or no value. It is very important to retain the original paint, lettering and decorations. Again, if you have significant doubts,

leave the piece alone. Advanced tin collectors know that even minor differences in finish, paint, and lettering can have a great impact on value.

When cleaning a tin collectible, it would probably be wise to avoid any flaked areas. Direct contact will generally create additional damage. If the inside of the tin container has significant rust, I recommend a small application of rust inhibitor. Your friendly hardware specialist can suggest a product. I have had good results with WD-40. I have spoken with several people in the business of restoring tins and Johnson's Paste Wax seems to be a favored product for that final wax application.

The large majority of tin containers have received heavy usage and will show scratches, dents, and some fading and discoloration. There are specialist restorers who can often remove the dents and scratches and blend in matching paint. Many collectors, however, enjoy the char-

*Honest Scrap Tobacco advertising sign after restoration. $775.00 – 1,250.00.* Courtesy of Chuck Kovacic.

acter that the years have added to a tin. Minor restoration can brighten up a tin. For example, filling in scratched areas with matching paint is preferable to refinishing a complete section. The decision to restore a tin should be based on the personal preference of the collector or dealer.

It is unfortunate that much of the damage to early tins and advertising items has been brought about by careless and improper handling, poor restoration efforts, and the application of a yellowing varnish or shellac. Tins should never be fully immersed in water. I would not recommend that steel wool or abrasive waxes be used. Tins and boxes with paper labels should be displayed or stored in areas without major temperature extremes or problems with humidity, mold, or fungus.

Other unanticipated damage can occur. I spent a few enjoyable hours at the home of Walter Neal, antique tin restorer of Wadsworth, Ohio. Walt showed me a Roly Poly tobacco tin that was missing the major portion of its paint. Walt explained that this highly desirable and scarce tin had once been in fine condition. The owner was transporting it and the tin had been placed in a plastic bag with little or no air entry, and left in the car for several hours. The day was very hot and humid. The combination of the intense heat and confining plastic bag caused the paint to react and literally peel off. What a disappointing discovery that must have been!

When transporting tins, it goes without saying that they should be individually wrapped to avoid contact and abrasion damage from other tins or objects. I prefer plain packing paper to newspaper. Some collectors tell me that newsprint can transfer to a tin or paper collectible.

## WOODEN CONTAINERS

Extreme care should be used in cleaning wooden containers. Wooden boxes with imprinting and no paper labels can be scrubbed with a mild detergent and a soft brush. Be careful not to apply too much direct pressure to the printed areas. There are non-yellowing varnish products on the market that may be applied after cleaning. My experience has been that most of these will darken the wood somewhat but as a bonus, will bring out the lettering bet-

ter. If you prefer, simply leave the box in the original condition after cleaning. The non-yellowing varnish, however, will prevent soiling and make the box easier to dust. It will also help preserve the wood.

## FRAMING & CARE OF OLD PAPER

Framing of choice advertising posters and related items should be done by an individual or retail framing service that is familiar with antique paper and has the awareness to handle it correctly and carefully. The framing should always utilize non-acid paper as a backing material. In addition and very important, there should be an air space between the glass and the actual advertising poster. I have seen a number of great posters over the years that were framed direct on the glass. A variety of conditions can cause the advertising piece to "bond" directly to the glass. One thing is for certain, once the bonding has taken place, any effort to remove the item from the frame will usually cause portions of the ad to remain on the glass. Framing an outstanding advertising poster as cheaply as possible is false economy.

Old paper is often extremely brittle and can be easily damaged by improper handling. Storage in damp basements or hot attics should be avoided. Significant damage to old paper should be repaired by an expert. Ron Schieber, a dealer in a variety of old paper items in Akron, Ohio, advised me that even small tears in advertising posters or other paper items should not be "repaired" with adhesive or non-adhesive tape. Ron states that he has seen instances of this type of tape leaving a residue on the paper, which he feels is not good.

Ron favors the use of wheat paste, which is also recommended by archivists. Ron also has used LePage's Mucilage but recommends caution when using this product. It can be removed if used properly.

I have seen significant water stains repaired on advertising posters as well as repairs made when a portion of the poster is missing. The repair work proved to be very satisfactory but a restoration specialist should be consulted for this specialized repair work. Again, the most important consideration is to not undertake repairs yourself if there is any doubt in your mind.

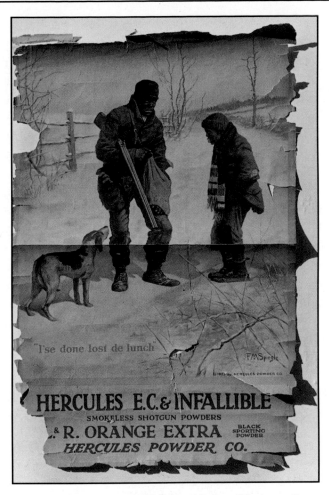

*Hercules E. C. & Infallible Smokeless Shotgun Powders. Hercules Powder Co. paper advertising sign. Substantial damage. Portions of the perimeter are missing.* Courtesy of Chuck Kovacic.

*Hercules Powder Co. poster after restoration. $225.00 – 450.00.* Courtesy of Chuck Kovacic.

## PROFESSIONAL RESTORATION

Professional restoration is available to collectors and dealers who possess an advertising item of inherent or special value to them. There are a number of people around the country who offer this service and they can generally be located through inquiry with museums, dealers, collector groups, and word of mouth. Some of these professionals can do some amazing things with a severely damaged item. I suggest that the collector make careful inquiry including, when possible, viewing examples of the restorer's work. I know of situations where collectors and dealers have utilized local artists with some very unpleasant results. Simply having art talent does not make one a qualified restorer.

I had the opportunity to interview a restorer who is active in the area of early advertising and is also a collector. The following question/answer session will hopefully provide some answers the reader may have about the restoration process. The reader should understand that I do not personally endorse or recommend any one individual. This is a decision that must be made by the individual collector or dealer.

Mr. Kovacic was kind enough to participate and provide photographs of some of his "before" and "after" work that illustrates what can be accomplished. As always, the decision must be made if the cost of restoration justifies the undertaking of the project. I have spoken to professional restorers and most seem to have their own unique approach to pricing. I do feel that competent restorers have a genuine pride in their workmanship and a primary concern to see a great advertising piece improved or returned to collectible condition and preservation.

*Mr. Wilson: What is your art background, technical training, special courses, etc.?*

Mr. Kovacic: My formal training comes from the Cleveland Institute of Art, where I earned a BFA in graphic design with a minor in photography/painting. Upon graduation in 1972, I worked as an art director/illustrator at several advertising agencies in the northern Ohio area. Later, I taught design production at the University of Akron. In 1982, I moved to southern California where I continued with my freelance graphic design and restoration work. Add to this a lot of time spent looking.

*Mr. Wilson: When did you begin to do restoration work? What stimulated your interest?*

Mr. Kovacic: I began my personal collection during my student days where I acquired many items that needed restoration. A close dealer friend, Bob Secrist, urged me to develop these skills. Soon, the curiosity of others became piqued. After that, word got to dealers fairly quickly concerning my abilities although many were reluctant to tell others of my talents. They wanted to keep me to themselves!

As an artist, I had always been attracted to early advertising items because of the quality of their illustrations, design, and printing. My training allowed me to appreciate and understand the production techniques used. Also, many of the early production houses for this work, most notably American Art Works and the Beech Company, were located in my area. Through contacts in the printing business, I

*De Laval Cream Separators. Large tin advertising sign. Before restoration. The sign shows uniform rusting sometimes called "pin spots." This condition is caused by moisture build-up and can substantially diminish the value of an otherwise great sign.* Courtesy of Chuck Kovacic.

*De Laval Cream Separators tin advertising sign after restoration. $1,250.00 – 2,600.00.* Courtesy of Chuck Kovacic.

had the privilege of speaking with surviving artists who had produced some of this work.

*Mr. Wilson: Do you have any special areas of interest? How do you locate items that interest you? What has been your most exciting acquisition?*

Mr. Kovacic: I've always been partial to cigar box labels and number over 1,500 different titles in my collection. The range of production techniques and illustration styles used offers a condensed history of printing and design. I often refer to my collection to determine a type style or technique.

I acquire items from dealers unaware of my abilities. Often, upon completion, they purchase these items back. Estate sales and flea markets have also provided many finds.

Recently, a collector brought me two "Chancellor Cigar" paper board signs. The illustration is a magnificent portrait of a woman, with *Chancellor* emblazoned upon her fan. Despite the efforts of another restorer, the dealer was convinced that nothing could be done to save them because of extensive water damage. He was so pleased with my completed work that he allowed me to keep one in payment. She now smiles down from my bedroom wall frustrating a number of collectors who have tried to buy her.

*Mr. Wilson: How long have you been offering your services to the antique advertising trade?*

My work started somewhat slowly in the mid seventies. Many of my first customers con-

*Chancellor Cigar paper advertising poster that was a victim of water damage.* Courtesy of Chuck Kovacic.

*The Chancellor cigar sign after restoration. $625.00 – 900.00.* Courtesy of Chuck Kovacic.

*A Conoco Gasoline porcelain sign that was the victim of target practice over the years.* Courtesy of Chuck Kovacic.

*The restored Conoco Gasoline sign. $275.00 – 425.00.* Courtesy of Chuck Kovacic.

tinue with me. I do my best to give them a quick turnaround time (8 to 12 weeks, sooner if needed for a show) and in almost 20 years of work, I've never lost a piece to the mails. Items are generally shipped UPS ground and insured for an amount determined by the client. My busy periods coincide with the Indianapolis, Indiana, Gaithersburg, Maryland, and Glendale, California, antique advertising shows.

*Mr. Wilson: What services do you offer?*

Mr. Kovacic: I work with metal signs, tobacco tins, trays, paper and cardboard, porcelain on metal, and metal and wood or plastic toys. I also have a source for professional silver and gold work and related restoration.

Often I'm asked to provide an appropriate frame for an item and always have a number of antique frames and new oak molding on hand. I do become involved with gesso work and just recently finished restoring the lettering and cattail motif on an early "Budweiser Girl" frame.

When appropriate, I have paper items professionally mounted on acid free museum board or rice paper. I do not de-acidify or bleach paper. I'm simply not set up to provide that service and I prefer the alternate method of painting out problem areas. This approach provides a more cost efficient and effective treatment for

my clients. Preference is to use water based paints, applying them with stippling technique that I've developed which mimics early stone-litho printing. When finished, I want to be unable to spot any of my restoration work from a distance greater than 24 inches.

Many of the items brought to me have had their lettering or product painted over or simply cut away by a previous owner interested only in the pretty picture. This was quite common during prohibition days with beer and whisky advertisements. Other items would be cut up by children for their scrap books. It becomes my task to determine the size and shape of those missing elements. Fortunately, I have an extensive research library and access to some top collections to verify and guide my replacement work.

A lot of items have simply been poorly manufactured. "Buster Brown Bread" metal signs are often pockmarked with rust because their faulty printing allowed moisture buildup between the metal and the printed surface. They require extensive restoration and rust removal but their pleasant subject matter makes the effort worthwhile.

Many early "roll-up" paper signs have been rolled and unrolled so many times that they become riddled with creases and torn and frayed in the process. I'm able to flatten much of that out and can replace the missing portions.

160

*Golden Sheaf Bakery, Manufacturers of Buster Brown Bread. This particular sign is often pockmarked with rust as a result of faulty printing which allowed moisture buildup between the metal and printed surface.* Courtesy of Chuck Kovacic.

*The restored Buster Brown tin sign. $350.00 – 500.00.* Courtesy of Chuck Kovacic.

A lot of fine porcelain signs are used as targets for people trying out their pistols. Fortunately, I've developed a technique to fill the bullet holes and replace the missing areas.

I've also had the pleasure of restoring the surface of cigar store Indians. Because of frequent trips to the Smithsonian and the Rockefeller Folk Art Collection in Williamsburg, Virginia, I've been able to conduct color and design research assuring a measure of accuracy.

But the most unusual piece that I've ever worked on was an 1888 assay safe. Its lettering and floral border needed replacement. It weighed a ton and required its owner to position it on his patio with a small crane!

*Mr. Wilson: What type of restoration work is the most difficult for you and why?*

Mr. Kovacic: I avoid reverse on glass and any stained glass items. This is a specialty unto itself. Indeed, there is a very competent artist in northern California who specializes in this work. Occasionally, I'm asked to work with original oil paintings. If the piece merits, I recommend that it be taken to a painting expert for proper chemical cleaning.

There are experts who actually reweave the fiber of the torn or missing paper back in place. This is an expensive and time consuming process and, accordingly, not always a viable alternative. It's not uncommon for a piece to be brought to me after it has been worked upon by another artist. In those cases, I have to reverse or improve earlier efforts.

Half-tone items pose a particularly vexing problem. This printing technique employs a fine dot or half-tone screen to print its image. Its use became the replacement for stone lithography starting after the first World War. On these items, the edge of any retouching is immediately visible because the restoration can't match the dot pattern used. I'm particularly frustrated with Coke trays dating from the mid twenties on because of this problem.

Because of their smaller size, tobacco tins require extra effort. And since these items invite closer inspection, my clients are more exacting in their requests.

*Mr. Wilson: What item have you done to date that was the biggest challenge? Why?*

Mr. Kovacic: A very rare "Moxie" sign was particularly challenging. It was riddled with nail holes and its embossed lettering had been flattened. Each hole had to be hammered out and the lettering re-embossed using special metal working tools. Extensive rust removal was involved, and I had to replace a missing corner.

Generally, when a piece is this damaged, I recommend that its owner write it off as a loss. Such a job simply becomes more my work than the original. But with an extremely rare sign such as this, complete restoration becomes a viable option. To avoid "making up" any missing pieces, it's critical to have a clear photo of a mint sign.

Since he was anxious to have this item in his inventory, the owner persuaded me that cost was no object. Familiar with my work, he teased that I might not be up to the task. I accepted his challenge. As you can see, it turned out

*Schlitz Beer self-contained tin advertising sign. Many of the old tin signs were saved over the years because of the beautiful lithographic art they contained. If some of the advertising proved to be objectionable, it was simply painted out. It appears that was the fate of this piece.* Courtesy of Chuck Kovacic.

rather nicely. However, the dealer got his revenge. He sent me a second, equally bad "Moxie" to restore!

*Mr. Wilson: What suggestions can you offer to collectors in the care and handling of the various forms of antique advertising: tin, paper, porcelain, metal, cardboard, trays? What can a reasonably competent collector do?*

Mr. Kovacic: The biggest mistake that people make is having their work restored by someone whose skills are not up to the task. As more people collect in this area of antiques, there are fewer mint pieces available. We wouldn't expect to buy a Ford Model T in mint condition, they don't exist. You have to look at the quality of the restoration work that's been done. All museums routinely restore their artworks and no one objects to restored Buddy-L toys. The same applies to antique advertising. The only resistance to restoration should be to resist bad restoration.

Paper and cardboard items should be backed with acid-free museum board available at better art supply stores. Never back these items with wood as it will leach into and discolor the paper. Many a sign has been ruined because it became stuck to the glass. The print should be separated from the glass with a liner or mat. Try to maintain your display area with a constant temperature. Be careful to hang the item out of direct sunlight and away from any heating/cooling vents, windows or doors. Once framed, never leave the item in direct sunlight. This is a problem for many dealers who display at outdoor shows. The power of the sun is magnified through the glass, allowing moisture to build up between the glass and the print. This allows fungus to attack your paper. We've all seen those telltale brown dots and foxing.

Never varnish a metal sign in an effort to bring back its original luster. These varnishes quickly decay, tinting the once clean surface brown. Even applying the varnish with a fine

*Schlitz Beer advertising sign after restoration. $575.00 – 1,250.00.* Courtesy of Chuck Kovacic.

*A very rare Moxie sign that appears as though it has suffered a variety of substantial damage.* Courtesy of Chuck Kovacic.

*A close-up of the Moxie sign displaying damage down to bare metal.* Courtesy of Chuck Kovacic.

*The restored Moxie sign. A similar Moxie sign had a reported auction price of $13,000.00.* Courtesy of Chuck Kovacic.

*A close-up of the Moxie restoration.* Courtesy of Chuck Kovacic.

brush leaves behind strokes. I've had no luck in removing any varnish. Try instead a high grade automotive polish, being careful to wipe away any excess polish to avoid white residue buildup. If a piece is heavily oxidized, every little crack and bump will become a collection point for this residue. *Never* polish an item that has been restored. You'll end up rubbing away the restoration work. The same applies to porcelain signs and trays.

Always begin with a clean surface, but be aware that cleaning can sometimes create problems. Wiping off an item with a damp cloth can mix tiny water particles with surface dust, causing further staining. Use a feather duster to remove any loose surface dirt, but be aware that if there is heavy flaking this light action could cause additional damage by snagging loose chips. This action can also cause additional dust and dirt to cling to the surface. With metal and porcelain signs, apply warm water with mild soap and then pat dry with a soft absorbent towel. Do so in even strokes in one direction. Avoid swirling or uneven pressure. Always begin at a corner to determine that cleaning will not remove or dull any remaining color.

If you've acquired a piece splattered with paint, you may be able to carefully scrape it off with an X-acto blade. You can also have some luck with 0000 steel wool. Avoid sandpapers since these quickly scratch through the paint surface and expose the metal. Solvents can sometimes be used. I often use Bestine solvent and thinner. Remember, however that if it can soften unwanted paint, it can do the same to the rest. Apply carefully with a Q-tip and have

plenty of clean towels on hand to absorb any excess. This requires patience and practice and is not for the faint of heart!

I also recommend that signs be framed. This allows for easier handling and offers protection to the edges and back. On larger prints, you may want to consider plexiglass instead of glass. Should your item drop as the result of an accident or earthquake, you won't have to deal with shards of glass which will damage your print and you. There are also products on the market to lessen ultraviolet damage.

*Mr. Wilson: How do you determine restoration prices? Supplied with a photo can you provide an accurate estimate or is it necessary to personally inspect the item?*

Mr. Kovacic: It's difficult to determine the extent of the work required from a photo. A photo won't tell me how brittle a piece is or its thickness. I need to inspect its surface area to determine the proper cleaning method. Also, when removing a sign from its frame, the edge will often reveal its original color. I also need to determine how much a piece has been cut down and the date of its printing. This information is too small to be revealed by any photo.

I have a minimum fee on all items. Since I never charge by the hour, I need to determine what value the owner places on a piece, its resale value and its rarity. Therefore, to assess my final fee, I try to determine the value that my restoration work is adding to a piece. Time wise, all my effort becomes an open-ended process. Because I'm also a collector, I work

*Get Fels-Naptha Here. Two-sided tin sign.* $115.00 – 165.00. Courtesy of Bob Brunswick.

until a piece is finished, treating each as if it were my own. I generally add a rush charge for clients anxious to have an item in time for a particular show or customer.

*Mr. Wilson: Do you feel that a customer should be advised when significant restoration work has been done?*

Mr. Kovacic: Absolutely. But as always, "caveat emptor" — let the buyer beware!

The reality is that many dealers aren't aware of my abilities and unknowingly pass along an item that they think has never been worked on. Not long ago a prominent dealer belittled my work, claiming that he never handled anything that had been restored. He didn't appreciate my pointing out that his most prized offering had received my attention.

Anxious to close a sale, many dealers will knowingly pass off items that I have worked on as "not restored." On the one hand, I accept this as a compliment to my abilities, but beyond recommending that my work be revealed, I have little control. When lettering has been completely added, I've begun to put a notice centered on the back announcing my work. That, you can look for, but it doesn't prevent someone from removing it. I also keep records of the items that I've worked on. The bottom line is that, I feel that as quality restoration becomes more available, we'll be more accepting of restoration work as a necessity and as an art.

I will tell you that I always try to keep my clients confidential. The items displayed here are done so with permission from their owners. Finally, make your purchases from reputable dealers whom you know and trust.

*Mr. Wilson: In your opinion...an original Honest Scrap board sign, in 10 mint condition, with a retail price of $1,000.00 is compared with a similar Honest Scrap with major problems being a 3. When restoration is completed, what would be your fee for bringing that up to a 9 level?*

Mr. Kovacic: Over the years I've worked on about a half dozen of this particular sign. Typically the board has begun to flake and break apart and has overall scratching and water damage. Collectors have always favored it because of its appealing image of a cat and dog confronting each other.

As always, an original should command the higher price. With the restoration that you described, I've seen this item fetch a price of $800.00 – $900.00. If we can accept that its unrestored dealer price was $50.00 – $100.00, my work would add $750.00 – $850.00 to its value. Remembering that I partially base my fees on the value that I add, my fee would be in the $300.00 – $400.00 range. This would allow room for the dealer to determine the final asking price. For a person keeping the piece for their collection and not interested in resale, the price of restoration becomes even more attractive. A much rarer sign requiring the same amount of work would, of course require a proportionately higher restoration fee.

In an ideal world, we would still have access to great mint signs. As more collectors enter this field though, fewer great pieces are available and at higher prices. This has afforded me the opportunity to save discarded items and allows others the opportunity to acquire items that might otherwise be unavailable. In that, I take great pleasure.

*Colgate's Octagon Soap. Offers a valuable premium coupon. $5.00 – 8.00 each.* Wilson Collection.

# Chapter Nine
## ⋯✦ A WORD TO COLLECTORS ✦⋯
### A Cornucopia of Collectibles from the Shelves, Counters, and Walls of the Old General Store

I've always felt that collecting should be fun and the source of considerable enjoyment. Often, the looking can be just as enjoyable as the acquiring. It is possible to assemble an impressive variety of country store antiques and there are numerous private collections. Natural enthusiasm should be controlled so that you do not find yourself spending the household expense money and owning items that will give no genuine pleasure.

If you are just starting out in this fascinating hobby, I strongly recommend that you visit museums, antique shops, auctions, recreated general stores, read the books and other publications that are available on the subject, and talk with other collectors. You will then be able to accept the validity of your own personal tastes and preferences and approach the hobby with great confidence.

It can be ultimately disappointing to think in terms of investment as you build your collection. Yes, it's true that many people have made substantial money from the later sale of their country store collectibles. The stories you often don't hear are those about the folks that paid too much and will either learn to live with the item or take a significant loss. For that reason it is wise to collect what you truly enjoy, but not overextend yourself in terms of time, effort, and financial outlay.

The collecting world has changed to an unbelievable degree since the beginning of my collecting days about 24 years ago. At that time, there seemed to be a lot of material available and, for the most part, the prices were reasonable. With heightened interest over the years and competition for desirable pieces advancing, the prices at the highest level have become astounding. A single tin container has been sold for more than $23,000.00, and a Campbell's Soup sign brought $93,500.00 at auction. In addition, a Kickapoo Indian Sagwa drug sign brought $55,000.00 at auction. Granted, these are extreme examples and only a few elite collectors have the resources to purchase these items. Unfortunately, it is no longer possible to

*5 Cent Counter. A tin sign that was frequently used in general stores to bring attention to the special bargain counter. $145.00 – 225.00.* Wilson Collection.

acquire an extensive collection of top quality country store memorabilia unless one has considerable money to spend.

I have in my files a country store collectibles price guide from 1970. How about these prices?

- ❧ Roll Top Desk: oak, original finish, 51" high and 53" wide. $200.00 – $300.00.
- ❧ Large Dayton Computing Platform Scale with highly decorative designs. $45.00.
- ❧ Diamond Inks Showcase Cabinet. $35.00.
- ❧ Diamond Dye Cabinet: good condition, depicting two children with balloon. $45.00.
- ❧ Wooden Coffee Bin: red paint with large stenciled lettering and design in gold on black, 22" high. $35.00.
- ❧ Glass Display Case: nickel-plated brass frame with wooden back door, cathedral top, 16" deep, 12" wide, and 35" high. $50.00.

By the way, these were dealer prices. With some looking, better prices could probably have been found.

With antiques and collectibles, there is no such thing as a catalog price or retail price. There is a range of prices. I have walked the aisles at numerous antique shows, as many of us have, only to discover an item in one dealer's booth for $125.00 and locate the same item in another dealer's booth in similar condition for $75.00. The price is set by what a willing seller will accept and what a willing purchaser is prepared to pay. Many elements can affect price: the eagerness of the collector to acquire the item, the motivation or financial situation of the seller, the knowledge of the seller, the scarcity and demand, and the list goes on.

It is true that a number of country store items have been sold frequently enough to provide a fairly good idea of value. Rare items are a completely different category. Many of these items show up at country store and advertising auctions and have brought amazing prices. The question remains regarding what these same pieces may fetch in the future.

Purchasing antiques is a skill that can be acquired. The more you know the better off you are. It remains also to understand that what appears high today could be a great bargain several years down the road. The trend for good country store material has been upward for sev-

eral years. The market can change as things come into favor or go out of favor. At present, pocket tobacco tins are very popular along with quality advertising signs and items. If you can't be satisfied with anything less than mint or excellent condition in what you purchase, your purchases will be less frequent and you will spend substantially more. On the other hand, if you are willing to accept imperfections and some damage, the field is wider and many of these items will look just about as good as their more expensive relatives as you display them in your collection. There are only so many mint and near-mint items to go around.

I would also suggest that when you find a piece you really like and can justify the purchase to your pocketbook, buy it on the spot. I include myself with a number of collectors who have found a great country store item at a show only to walk away and look further to give it some more thought. Lo and behold when we return, that tobacco tin or advertising sign we pictured in our collection was gone.

Finding a true bargain in today's market is much more difficult than it was in the past. The age of information is with us and people are much more aware of values. In fact, it can be much easier to pay a fair price to a dealer than to attempt to buy from an individual. The non-dealer may have seen an item "just like mine" sell for $500.00 but not give proper credit for condition or type. Even closely related items do not necessarily have similar value.

## SOURCES OF COUNTRY STORE MATERIAL

Good sources for country store material are just about anywhere, but some sources are better than others. I have found very collectible items at garage sales, estate sales, and for sale by private individuals. Responding to ads such as those found in the *Antique Trader* can prove to be worthwhile. Beyond antique shops, there are some great specialty shows and flea markets. Attending major advertising shows such as those held at Indianapolis, Indiana; Gaithersburg, Maryland; and Glendale, California; can be very exciting. You will see more advertising and country store items at a specialty show than you can possibly see by visiting numerous antique shops. Be aware of the fact that considerable selling and horse-trading generally goes

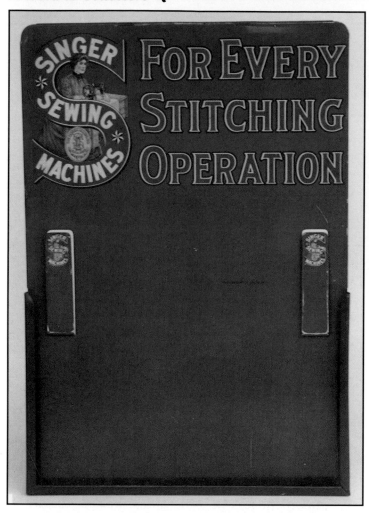

*Singer Sewing Machines. For Every Stitching Operation. Tin calendar sign with slots for the day and month. $175.00 – 250.00.* Wilson Collection.

on before the doors are open to the public. A tin container, for example, may pass through the hands of several dealers before a two-day show concludes.

There are also some major flea markets that offer considerable merchandise and the opportunity to make a "find." Some of these are held in Brimfield, Massachusetts; Kutztown, Pennsylvania; Phoenix, Arizona; Columbus, Ohio; Ann Arbor, Michigan; and Charlotte, North Carolina; among many others. Look for advertised flea markets in your area and plan to attend — you can have an enjoyable time, meet some interesting people, and perhaps make a great addition to your collection.

Horse-trading with other collectors and dealers can be the source of some real treasures. Generally, you are wise to trade for items of comparable value or rarity. There can be a great temptation to accept ten or so relatively common tobacco tins, for example, in exchange for your scarce tin. As your collecting skills and tastes become refined, the wisdom of retaining your best collectibles will be demonstrated. However, very good trades with satisfaction by both parties can be made when trading like value for like value.

*Detail of the advertising portion of the Singer sign.* Wilson Collection.

*Two trade cards advertising Standard Screw Fastened Boots and Shoes and Golden Soap, Empire Soap Co., St. Louis. It appears that this gentleman values the soap more than money! $2.00 – 6.00.* Wilson Collection.

### AUCTIONS

Auctions can be a great source of good country store material. The three major rules are:

1. Arrive early for the auction preview.

2. Closely inspect the items you are interested in three times or even more to make certain you are satisfied with authenticity and condition.

3. Jot down the maximum price you are willing to pay and do not exceed that price.

It can help to have a friend along to provide you with additional knowledge, advice, and counsel.

The quality of auctions can range from top-level, fine quality specialized auctions to those that include a few desirable pieces and mostly second and third-class merchandise. Auctions can provide spectacular bargains but can also sell you overpriced junk. Auctions are usually the quickest way of liquidating an estate, collection, or other saleable collectibles.

Again, the more knowledge you have, the better off you are. I cannot emphasize enough that you should closely examine anything you intend to bid on. Be certain that you know what you are purchasing. It is a good idea to sit up front so the auctioneer can easily see you and be aware of your bid. It can be very disappointing to have your bids missed. This will also permit you to see all of the merchandise as the auction progresses.

Bid quickly and clearly, and remember that once the auctioneer says "sold" the item is yours. Don't get a bad case of "auction fever"

*Roger's Grocery. An early wooden sign that was found during an excavation project in Corona, California. $95.00 – 175.00.* Wilson Collection.

and bid far beyond the value of an item. I have seen perfectly intelligent and otherwise reasonable people get caught up in the excitement of the moment and pay substantially more for a piece than they would even consider if that same collectible were discovered in an antique shop.

Be certain that you understand the specific rules of the auction and the terms of payment. When attending auctions, basic words of wisdom are "buyer beware." If you have any doubts about the authenticity of an item or if the bids exceed reasonable value, don't bid! I guess the exception is when you find that your enthusiasm for ownership exceeds other factors.

There are a growing number of specialty country store and advertising auctions around the country and they are always interesting to attend. Some incredible private collections have been sold in this manner. These auctions are generally heavily advertised and will provide illustrated and descriptive information if requested.

May good fortune be with you at the auctions you attend. If you know the reasonable value of what you are buying and stick to your agreed figure, you can't go too wrong.

## DISPOSING OF YOUR COLLECTION

For many of us, that fateful day will come when we wrestle with the decision to sell all or a portion of our collection. There are emotional issues to deal with as well as the financial ones. In addition to what they represent, collectibles also are memories of places and locations and good times, of long bargaining sessions and serious horse-trades. Collections are disposed of for a variety of reasons: ill health, death, divorce, financial needs, space and storage problems, or simply because one has enjoyed the collection and prices have advanced substantially.

If you plan to dispose of a collection of country store memorabilia, you should look at dealers, individuals, and auction houses that specialize in this material. They generally know the market and can provide a fair idea of ultimate sale price. Simply calling up the local antique shop or placing an ad in the paper will usually not gain the best price. If a dealer specializes in glassware, antique dolls or furniture, is it likely that they have the knowledge and market to sell your items at a strongly favorable price and thereby pay you a good price?

If you are disposing of all or a large portion of your collection, it is most often wise to sell it as a unit. You will frequently have the opportunity to individually sell your very choice items. But by doing this, the overall appeal of your collection will be greatly diminished in the eyes of an auction house or knowledgeable dealer. The highly desirable items in your collection can help carry the less desirable ones when selling to a dealer or contracting to an auction house.

If you have just a few items to sell, dealers who specialize in country store Americana can be a good source. From time to time, I have sold various items to dealers because I have found a relatively expensive single item that I wanted to purchase. I was paid a fair price for my collectibles by the dealer and often the dealer was able to sell the items he purchased by making a few phone calls.

Collecting country store material can provide a considerable amount of satisfaction. The thrill of discovering something new to add to your collection is a wonderful feeling. Country store collectors represent all walks of life, but we all share great enthusiasm for general store collectibles! As long as there are collectors, the lights of the old general store will never grow dim. Please enjoy the cornucopia of old store material that follows.

*Three celluloid mirrors. Left, $18.00 – 35.00. The middle one advertises Mennen's Violet Talcum Toilet Powder, $35.00 – 75.00. Right, $18.00 – 35.00.* Wilson Collection.

*An early coffee mill, $155.00 – 250.00, and spice container, $85.00 – 130.00.* Courtesy of Bob Brunswick.

*Bouquet Coffee tins, O.V. Tracy & Co., Syracuse, N.Y. $55.00 – 75.00 each.* Courtesy of Bob Brunswick.

*A set of allspice & ginger shelf caddies. Very colorful and great condition. $175.00 – 325.00.*
Courtesy of Bob Brunswick.

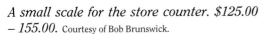

*A small scale for the store counter. $125.00 – 155.00.* Courtesy of Bob Brunswick.

A spice container illustrated with a parrot, $70.00 – 90.00, and a tea container illustrated with an elk, $85.00 – 130.00. Great Atlantic & Pacific Tea Company. Courtesy of Bob Brunswick.

Two early coffee grinders for the home. The one on the right advertises None Such Mincemeat, $155.00 – 250.00. Left, $85.00 – 145.00. Courtesy of Bob Brunswick.

The Old Settler Clears Black Rainwater. Cardboard. $8.00 – 15.00. Wilson Collection.

A delightful scene of a beautiful girl holding a candle and thinking about Santa Claus. 1893. A Christmas card placed in each package of coffee during the Christmas season. Woolson *Spice Co.*, Toledo, Ohio. $25.00 – 45.00. Wilson Collection.

*Santa Claus himself. Woolson Spice Co., Toledo, Ohio. 1891. $25.00 – 45.00.* Wilson Collection.

*The illustrated back of a Lion Coffee card by The Woolson Spice Company of Toledo, Ohio.* Wilson Collection.

*Old Kris Kringle with his reindeer. Another beautiful card that was placed in Lion Coffee during the holidays. 1890. $25.00 – 45.00.* Wilson Collection.

*Jack-In-The-Box with a Christmas scene. Lion Coffee. Woolson Spice Company, Toledo, Ohio. Youngsters were encouraged to collect the entire set. To do this, Mom and Dad had to purchase Lion Coffee. 1890. $12.00 – 20.00.* Wilson Collection.

*A very large and unusual "tub container" from a general store in Doylestown, Ohio. These were used to display a variety of products. Scarce. $425.00 – 650.00.* Wilson Collection.

*Genuine English Fruit Cake tin container. United States Baking Company. A beautiful tin illustrated with an American eagle. $45.00 – 75.00.* Courtesy of Bob Brunswick.

*A die-cut stand-up counter ad for Blue Label Tomato Ketchup. Curtice Brothers Co., Rochester, N. Y. $60.00 – 95.00.* Wilson Collection.

*A display caddy with glass front. Manufactured by J. J. Utted Co., Buffalo, New York. $45.00 – 75.00.* Courtesy of Bob Brunswick.

*A paper bag with wood-cut of the store delivery wagon. F. B. Gates Grocer, Plymouth, Connecticut. $8.00 – 12.00.* Wilson Collection.

*A large advertising trade card for Phenix Insurance Company. $5.00 – 12.00.* Wilson Collection.

*Hood's Sarsaparilla calendar for 1896. $55.00 – 85.00.* Wilson Collection.

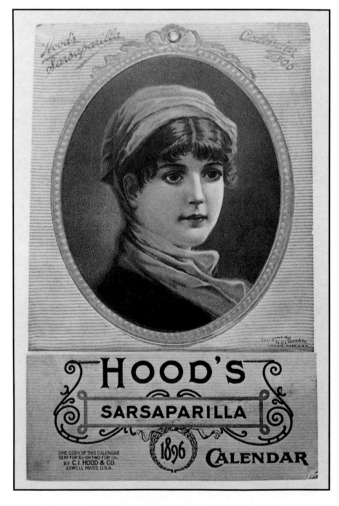

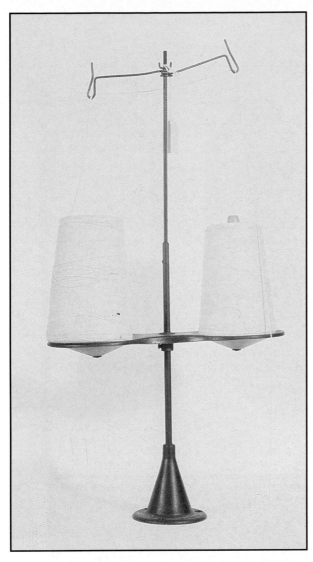

Die-cut card illustrating Easter rabbits. From the London Clothing Co., Los Angeles, California. 1895. $12.00 – 16.00. Wilson Collection.

General store string holder. Iron and wire. $95.00 – 120.00. Wilson Collection.

Wiss Shears and Scissors heavy paper advertising sign. $55.00 – 85.00. Wilson Collection.

An allspice store caddy illustrated with a pretty lady. $150.00 – 225.00. Courtesy of Bob Brunswick.

Family Tea container and Finest Teas & Coffees. Norwalk, Ohio. Left, $85.00 – 130.00. Right, $45.00 – 90.00. Courtesy of Bob Brunswick.

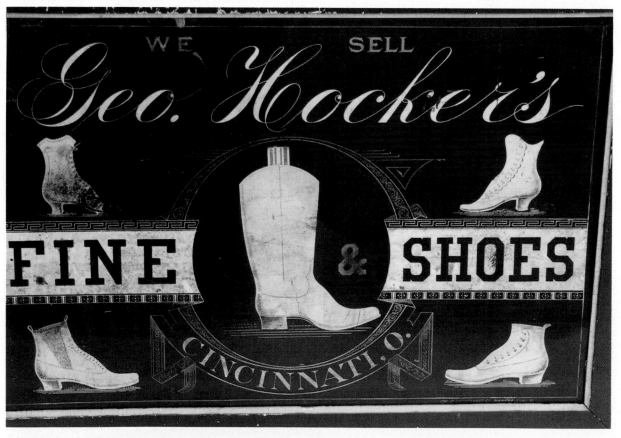

We Sell Geo. Hocker's Fine Boots & Shoes tin advertising sign. A very early sign. $550.00 – 875.00. Wilson Collection.

*N. L. Co. Lozenges tin container with glass front, and a tea container. Left, $55.00 – 100.00. Right, $85.00 – 130.00.* Courtesy of Bob Brunswick.

*Pure Maple Syrup, $27.00 – 42.00; coffee, $45.00 – 75.00; and a Runkel Brothers Breakfast Cocoa tin, $38.00 – 65.00.* Courtesy of Bob Brunswick.

*Samovar Uncolored Teas. Store shelf caddy. $75.00 – 125.00.* Courtesy of Bob Brunswick.

*Pastime Plug Tobacco. One of the most beautifully illustrated tobacco containers. The inside lid features a man with his jumping horse. The top of the tin shows a hunter shooting at some birds. A bird is falling from the sky and hunter's dog is at his side. This tin was a store counter display and held 18 pounds of tobacco. Made at the Ginna plant in the 1890's. $250.00 – 425.00.* Courtesy of Bob Brunswick.

*Clark's O.N.T. Spool Cotton trade card. Depicts a cowboy lassoing a longhorn steer. $5.00 – 8.50.* Wilson Collection.

*This beautiful illustration of a little girl with spectacles reading a book was a stock print and used frequently for a variety of advertising. I found this one in Maine several years ago. $225.00 – 375.00.* Wilson Collection.

*A large card advertising the Stover Bicycle Manufacturing Co. Illustrated with a large number of Brownies. $25.00 – 45.00.* Wilson Collection.

*A set of cards that was handed out by Gross Bros., Tacoma, Wash. The children are taking their bath and preparing for bed. $4.00 – 7.50 per card.* Wilson Collection.

*Balm of Tulips. A reliable remedy sold by druggists and country stores for 25¢ per bottle. Dr. Robinson, Foxcroft, Maine. $15.00 – 25.00.* Wilson Collection.

*The other two cards in the set. $4.00 – 7.50 per card.* Wilson Collection.

*A piece of "scrap" that was probably handed out by some early-day store and carefully preserved in a book. $2.00 – 4.00.* Wilson Collection.

*An advertising card for Metropolitan Life Insurance Company, quaint illustration of a girl in red holding a chicken. 1893. There is a solicitation on the back for new agents. $9.00 – 15.00.* Wilson Collection.

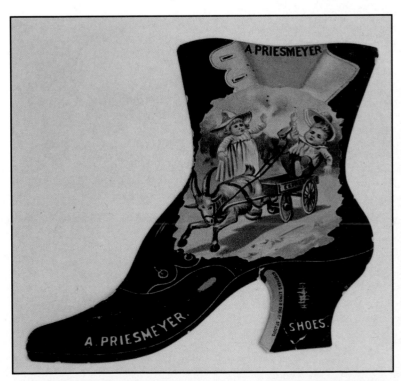

*A celluloid brush from Fred C. Bishop, lumber and coal dealer of Centerburg, Ohio. 1900. $27.00 – 45.00.* Wilson Collection.

*A. Priesmeyer Shoes. Die-cut advertising card with a quaint child's scene. $6.00 – 12.00.* Wilson Collection.

185

*"An Old Fashioned New England Grocery."* This print was given to storekeepers with the compliments and hope for continued patronage. Chase and Sanborn Coffee, 1897. $525.00 – 750.00. Wilson Collection.

*Ayer's Cherry Pectoral die-cut Santa Claus. This is a stand-up ad and was often placed on the counter or shelf of the drug section.* $200.00 – 325.00. Wilson Collection.

# ·•✧ BIBLIOGRAPHY ✧•·

Atherton, Lewis. *Main Street on the Middle Border*. Bloomington, Indiana: Indiana University Press, 1954.

Beck, Doreen. *Collecting Country & Western Americana*. New York: The Hamlyn Publishing Group, 1975.

Berger, Michael L. *The Devil Wagon in God's Country: The Automobile and Social Change in Rural America, 1893 – 1929*. Hamden, Connecticut: Archon Books, 1979.

Carson, Gerald. *The Old Country Store*. New York: Oxford University Press, 1954.

Carson, Gerald. *One for a Man, Two for a Horse: A Pictorial History, Grave & Comic, of Patent Medicines*. Garden City, New York: Doubleday & Company, Inc., 1961.

Clark, Hyla M. *The Tin Can Book*. New York: New American Library, 1977.

Clark, Thomas D. *Pills, Petticoats, & Plows: The Southern Country Store*. Norman, Oklahoma: University of Oklahoma Press, 1944 (third printing 1989).

Cohn, David L. *The Good Old Days*. New York: Simon and Schuster, 1940.

Dary, David. *Entrepreneurs of the Old West*. New York: Alfred A. Knopf, 1986.

Davidson, Marshall B. *Life in America, Volumes I & II*. Boston, Massachusetts: Houghton Mifflin Company, 1951.

Dolan, J.R. *The Yankee Peddlers of Early America*. New York: Clarkson N. Potter, Inc., 1964.

Haggard, Howard W., M.D. *Devils, Drugs, and Doctors*. New York: Blue Ribbon Books, Inc., 1929.

Heimann, Robert K. *Tobacco & Americans*. New York: McGraw Hill Book Company, Inc., 1960.

Holbrook, Stewart H. *The Golden Age of Quackery*. New York: The Macmillan Company, 1959.

Johnson, Laurence A. *Over the Counter and on the Shelf, Country Storekeeping in America, 1620 – 1920*. Rutland, Vermont: Charles E. Tuttle Company, Publishers, 1961.

Karolevitz, Robert F. *Doctors of the Old West*. New York: Bonanza Books, 1967.

Lingeman, Richard. *Small Town America, A Narrative History, 1620 – The Present*. New York: G.P. Putnam's Sons, 1980.

National Geographic Book Service. *We Americans*. Washington, D.C.: National Geographic, 1976.

Needham, Walter and Mussey, Barrows. *A Book of Country Things*. Brattleboro, Vermont: The Stephen Greene Press, 1965.

Pearson, Haydn S. *Countryman's Year*. New York: McGraw Hill Book Company, Inc., 1949.

Rifkind, Carole. *Main Street: The Face of Urban America*. New York: Harper Colophon Books, 1977.

Roberts, Bruce and Jones, Ray. *American Country Stores*. Chester, Connecticut: The Globe Pequot Press, 1991.

Rockmore, Cynthia and Julian. *The Country Auction Antiques Book*. New York: Hawthorn Books, Inc., 1974.

Rowsome, Frank Jr. *They Laughed When I Sat Down: An Informal History of Advertising in Words and Pictures*. New York: Bonanza Books, 1959.

Sandler, Martin W. *This Was America*. Boston, Massachusetts: Little, Brown & Company, 1980.

Schroeder, Joseph J., Editor. *Reproduction of the Sears Roebuck & Co. Catalog for Fall 1900*. Northfield, Illinois: Digest Books, 1970.

Time Life Books. *This Fabulous Century 1870 – 1900*. New York: Time Life Publishing, 1970.

Time Life Books. *This Fabulous Century 1900 – 1910*. New York: Time Life Publishing, 1969.

Wheeler, Keith (text by). *The Old West Series: The Townsmen*. New York: Time, Inc., 1975.

Wilson, Everett B. *Vanishing America*. New York: A.S. Barnes & Co., Inc., 1961.

Young, James Harvey. *The Toadstool Millionaires: A Social History of Patent Medicines in America Before Federal Regulations*. Princeton: Princeton University Press, 1972.

# COLLECTOR GROUPS, MAGAZINES, & OTHER PUBLICATIONS OF INTEREST

Tin Container Collectors Association
Box 440101
Aurora, Colorado 80044
Publication: *Tin Type*

Antique Advertising Association of America
P.O. Box 1121
Morton Grove, Illinois 60053
Publication: *Past Times*

American Game Collectors Association
49 Brooks Avenue
Lewiston, Maine 04246

The Ephemera Society of America
P.O. Box 37
Schoharie, New York 12157

Trade Card Collectors Association
Box 284
Marlton, New Jersey 08053

National Association of Paper &
  Advertising Collectors
P.O. Box 500
Mount Joy, Pennsylvania 17552
Publication: *P.A.C. (The Paper and
  Advertising Collector)*

*Collectors' Showcase*
5200 S. Yale, 7th Floor
Tulsa, Oklahoma 74135

*Antique Toy World*
P.O. Box 34509
Chicago, Illinois 60634

*Antique Review*
P.O. Box 538
Worthington, Ohio 43085-0538

*The Antique Trader Weekly*
P.O. Box 1050
Dubuque, Iowa 52001-1050

*Antiques & Auction News*
P.O. Box 500
Mount Joy, Pennsylvania 17552

*Mountain States Collector*
P.O. Box 2525
Evergreen, Colorado 80439

*Dolls, The Collector's Magazine*
Collector Communications Corporation
170 5th Avenue
New York, NY 10010-5911

*Collectors News & The Antique Reporter*
P.O. Box 156
Grundy Center, Iowa 50638-0156

*The American Collectors Journal*
P.O. Box 407
Kewanee, Illinois 61443-0407

*Collectibles — Country & Americana*
GCR Publishing Group, Inc.
1700 Broadway
New York, NY 10019

*The New York Antique Almanac*
P.O. Box 335
Lawrence, New York 11559-9830

*Midwest Antique & Collectible News*
P.O. Box 529
Anna, Il 62906

*Maine Antique Digest*
P.O. Box 1429
Waldoboro, Maine 04572-1429

*The Mid Atlantic Antiques Magazine*
P.O. Box 908
Henderson, N.C. 27536

# MUSEUMS, DEALERS, COLLECTORS, RESTORATION SERVICES, & STORES

Harold Warp Pioneer Village
Minden, Nebraska
(Fascinating complex includes The Peoples Store — a complete old-time general store.)

Shelburne Museum
Shelburne, Vermont
(Plan to spend a day here. An incredible display of Early Americana including The Tuckaway General Store & Apothecary Shop. Exhibit includes a great variety of old-time country store items.)

Kansas State Historical Society
120 West Tenth
Topeka, Kansas

Alaska State Library & Museum
Juneau, Alaska

Twinsburg Historical Society
Twinsburg, Ohio

Ohio State Historical Society & Museum
Columbus, Ohio

Mariposa Museum & History Center
Mariposa, California
(Museum exhibit features the Gagliardo Store which was established in Hornitos, California in 1854. The store was owned and operated by members of the family until 1960.)

American Advertising Museum
9 NW Second Avenue
Portland, Oregon

Knott's Berry Farm
Buena Park, California
(Knott's Ghost Town has a working general store with a number of artifacts on display.)

Vermont Country Store
Weston, Vermont
(An old-time store selling goods of today and yesteryear. Many early store items on display.)

California State Parks
Bodie Ghost Town
Bodie, California
(Includes an original general store containing old merchandise.)

Calico Ghost Town
Calico, California
(Developed by Walter Knott of Knott's Berry Farm, this historical mining town is open to the public and includes an old general store.)

Cheap John's Country Store
John & Mary Jo Purdum
104 South Main Street
Waynesville, Ohio
(John & Mary Jo operate an antiques business and also have on display their wonderful collection of country store Americana. The exhibit is open to the public and should not be missed if you happen to be in the area.)

South Park City
Fairplay, Colorado
(An authentic restoration of an early pioneer mining town which includes Simpkin's General Store.)

Mad Money
Ron Schieber
1867 West Market Street
Akron, Ohio 44313
(Dealer in quality ephemera.)

Antique Cash Registers
William J. Navratil
8636 Wyatt Road
Broadview Heights, Ohio 44147

Patrice McFarland
Box 161
Averill Park, New York 12018
(Board game collector and very knowledgeable about early games.)

Chuck Kovacic
14383 b Nordhoff
Panorama City, California 91402-1927
(Offers restoration services for tin, paper, metal, cardboard, and porcelain.)

Walter Neal
Tin Restorer
Wadsworth, Ohio

Archival Restoration Associates
P.O. Box 1395
North Wales, Pennsylvania 19454

Old Print Shop
150 Lexington Avenue
New York, NY 10016

Paper Collectors' Marketplace
P.O. Box 12899
Scandinavia, Wisconsin 54977

Bumpas Emporium & Drugstore
10 Tallmadge Circle
Tallmadge, Ohio 44278

Cass Country Store
Cass, West Virginia
(At one time, perhaps the largest company store in America. Sells gifts and souvenirs. Established in 1902.)

Mast General Store
Valle Crucis, North Carolina
(Est. 1892. A great old-time country store to visit.)

Virginia City General Store
Virginia City, Montana
(Located in a historic area that dates to the Montana gold-rush era. A museum with some great store items on display.)

Oldest Store Museum in America
St. Augustine, Florida
(Store museum with thousands of artifacts on display.)

Living History Farms
Walnut Hills, Iowa
(A living history museum with an 1870's general store.)

Asa Knight Store
Old Sturbridge Village
Sturbridge, Massachusetts
(This interesting store was established in the 1830's and operated until 1863. Part of a fabulous living history museum complex.)

# Schroeder's ANTIQUES Price Guide

. . . is the #1 best-selling antiques & collectibles value guide on the market today, and here's why . . .

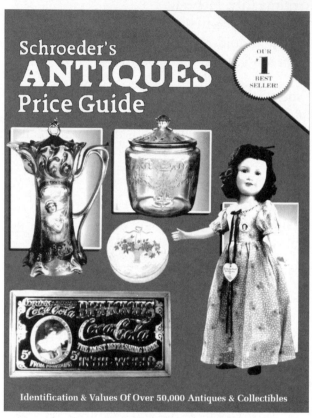

*Schroeder's*
**ANTIQUES**
Price Guide

OUR #1 BEST SELLER!

Identification & Values Of Over 50,000 Antiques & Collectibles

*8½ x 11, 608 Pages, $12.95*

- *More than 300 advisors, well-known dealers, and top-notch collectors work together with our editors to bring you accurate information regarding pricing and identification.*

- *More than 45,000 items in almost 500 categories are listed along with hundreds of sharp original photos that illustrate not only the rare and unusual, but the common, popular collectibles as well.*

- *Each large close-up shot shows important details clearly. Every subject is represented with histories and background information, a feature not found in any of our competitors' publications.*

- *Our editors keep abreast of newly-developing trends, often adding several new categories a year as the need arises.*

---

If it merits the interest of today's collector, you'll find it in *Schroeder's*. And you can feel confident that the information we publish is up to date and accurate. Our advisors thoroughly check each category to spot inconsistencies, listings that may not be entirely reflective of market dealings, and lines too vague to be of merit. Only the best of the lot remains for publication.

Without doubt, you'll find
**SCHROEDER'S ANTIQUES PRICE GUIDE**
the only one to buy for
reliable information and values.

**COLLECTOR BOOKS**
*A Division of Schroeder Publishing Co., Inc.*